G

Interne'

& You

God,
Internet Church
& You

by

Davo Roberts

Acknowledgements

Editing & Proofing: Roger Kirby

God, Internet Church & You – version 1.5

Text & Graphics Copyright © 2020 Dave G Roberts

ISBN-13: 978-1505963458
ISBN-10: 1505963451

All images are in greyscale rather than full colour for the purpose of reducing the price of the book.

Contents

Introduction

As the Church continues through the twenty-first century, technology as ever marches inexorably onwards. Into this, the way Church operates has also adapted. This is where the Church does not meet in a specific physical location but gathers in what is called the internet or as it is also known as, "Digital Space". Therefore, Internet Church is sometimes referred to as Digital Church. Some questions we will seek to answer in this book are:

- What is the Internet?
- Can God really interact within an Internet Environment'?
- What is an Internet Church?
- How does an Internet Church function?
- What are the virtues and liabilities of an Internet Church?
- Can an Internet Church be considered part of the historical Church?
- How can this technology be used so that Christians can be discipled effectively in the twenty-first century and beyond?

Internet Church is only just beginning in real terms within the 2,000 years of Church History. As technologies evolve and their use becomes ever increasingly widespread, the Church of Jesus Christ needs to adapt consistently. A simple question to start our thinking with before we go further.

How are we to use the internet? With imagination. Simply because you can't think of a way to do something, doesn't mean somebody else can't also. Just because we or others don't understand something, does not mean it is necessarily wrong or even sinful. We shouldn't limit ourselves, as Church, as Christians, simply because our individual & collective imagination is limited. An historical event which is a good example of this "limited imagination" are the protests when Johannes Gutenberg invented the printing press in the 15th century. This is in order that it remains 'one, holy, catholic and apostolic body', constantly engaging in fellowship, worship, mission and bible teaching. The Church can use Digital Space in particular, to enable and embrace those who are unable to get to traditional forms of Church. These people are those who for physical, psychological or geographical reasons, are unable to attend or be involved in Church. The Church needs to be open to all – including those unable to physically attend.

Using Digital Space, isolated Churches, communities, families and individuals will be enabled and to meet in a 'Internet Church'. This will lead to Jesus Christ, who is the head of the Church, being glorified. Overall, the Internet Church will not supplant the local physical Church but will rather harmonize with it.

However, if a person can get to a traditional physical Church, then they probably should attend that Church and be involved there as well as at an Internet Church. The Internet Church is one part of the "one, holy, catholic and apostolic Church". An exciting future lies ahead for the Universal Church to which we continue to cry together: "Come Lord Jesus! Come".

It should also be noted that the internet can also be an ideal way for people to develop and exercise their innate creativity and spiritual gifts. Ways including blogging, social media, video and audio. We look at that together in Section 3. However, first let us have a look at what a Church, any Church, must be like if it is to fit in with biblical guidelines.

Section 1:

What does the Bible say about Church?

1.1. What Is The Church?

[13] When Jesus came to the region of Caesarea Philippi, he asked His disciples, 'Who do people say the Son of Man is?'
[14] They replied, 'Some say John the Baptist; others say Elijah; and still others, Jeremiah or one of the prophets.'
[15] 'But what about you?' he asked. 'Who do you say I am?'
[16] Simon Peter answered, 'You are the Messiah, the Son of the living God.'
[17] Jesus replied, 'Blessed are you, Simon son of Jonah, for this was not revealed to you by flesh and blood, but by my Father in heaven. [18] And I tell you that you are Peter, and on this rock, I will build my church, and the gates of Hades will not overcome it. [19] I will give you the keys of the kingdom of heaven; whatever you bind on earth will be bound in heaven, and whatever you loose on earth will be loosed in heaven.' [20] Then he ordered His disciples not to tell anyone that he was the Messiah. (Matthew 16:13-20)

The Biblical word 'Church' comes from the word 'ekklesia' or 'assembly' and means a group of people called out to God by God. However, it can mean rather different things. There is the Universal Church, or the invisible Church, which is all believers, of all time, whether living or with the Lord. This is the body of Christ. This is the Church in the universal sense when the Bible talks about the entire body of Christ.

Then we have the local Church, which we know as the visible Church, the body of Christ in action in the world, as referred to by Paul (Romans 16:3-5). This second aspect is used within the confines of the local congregation, such as the Thessalonian Church (1 Thessalonians 1:1). In the New Testament, the word 'Church' has a dual meaning, depending on context, of either the universal (invisible) or local (visible), attached to it. It is a nuance not found within the English translations. While the visible Church comprises local communities of believers, the invisible Church is the entire fellowship of members of the family of God. Only God knows who members of the invisible Church are. However, the visible Church can be seen through local faith communities.

Lastly, there is Christ's Church, looking back to Jesus' statement of authority "I will build my Church" (Matthew 16:18). For indeed, Jesus is building His Church, because Jesus Christ is the head of the Church and the Church is the body. Jesus Christ alone is the head to whom the Church, all Christians, are to submit to His leadership, unity and authority (Ephesians 1:22-23). Jesus Christ is the Lord of the Church and the Church is to be obedient to Him as He sustains, guides and blesses the Church. Jesus Christ will be coming back one day to collect all those who are authentically His Church – all those who down through time have submitted their life to Him as the one Way to the Father. Does that include you?

The phrase 'one holy, catholic and apostolic Church' probably remains the best means of identifying whether a Church is truly part of the historical Church or not. The Church at its establishment was a practice of shared faith, identified by four dynamic hallmarks: One, Holy, Catholic and Apostolic. Therefore, if any Church does not bear all four of these hallmarks, then it cannot be a true Church of Jesus Christ. Why is that? Simply because these hallmarks have been accepted for centuries throughout the different strands of historical Christianity. Although definitions may vary, these four hallmarks, cover the broad spectrum of historical Christendom, within the Orthodox, Roman Catholic and Protestant Churches.

The Purpose of the Church

If that is what Church is, we naturally go on to ask what is the purpose of the Church. Scripture tells us that the purpose of the Church, is to glorify God (Ephesians 3:10, 21), to build up God's people through to spiritual maturity (Ephesians 4:12-13), equip God's people for service (Ephesians 4:11-13), to evangelise by telling others about Jesus Christ (Matthew 28:19) and to promote the spiritual and physical welfare of all people, of all nations and time, whether they are in the Church or not (Galatians 6:10).

The Church and Jesus

The relationship of the Church with her master, Jesus Christ can be summed up in a combination of 3 ways.

The Church is the Body of Christ: That is the Church is a living organism and not merely an organization (Ephesians 1:22-23, 4:15-16). All Christians are baptized into one body, the Universal Church, (1 Corinthians 12:13) and this body is made up of many parts or believers. Each part or believer has a vitally necessary and important function to perform to the glory of God (Ephesians 4:15; 1 Corinthians 12:13).

The Church is the Bride of Christ: This suggests the purity, holiness and faithfulness that should be the hallmark of God's people. Furthermore, it suggests the great love that Jesus Christ has for His Church, the Bride (2 Corinthians 11:2; Ephesians 5:25-32; Revelation 19:7, Revelation 22:17).

The Church is the Temple of Christ: Jesus Christ is building a spiritual temple with Himself as the Cornerstone or foundation stone. Christian Disciples, followers of Jesus Christ, are living stones and God dwells within the temple, filling it with all His fullness (Ephesians 2:22; 1 Peter 2:5).

Church Government

The Church was intended to be governed by elders (or bishops) and deacons and these were appointed by the apostles in the New Testament Churches in order to govern the Church, therefore by leading, administering discipline and teaching believers (Hebrews 13:17; 1 Timothy 5:17). Today, there are three main forms of Church government systems operating, all of which lay claim to having some form of Biblical precedence.

Congregational (Baptist, Brethren Etc.): This stresses the autonomy and independence of the local Church, with each local Church is answerable only to Jesus Christ as its head (Acts 13:1–3). Elders and deacons are elected or appointed by the local Church and promote the priesthood of all believers. There may be support bodies to liaise between similar Churches. The variety of practices in the early Church suggests that there isn't a need to be bound to any one practice, but use the most appropriate for that situation.

Episcopalian (Anglican, Roman Catholics, Orthodox): This is a hierarchical system of Church government consisting of Archbishops, bishops and priests, which governs the denomination. Reasons for this include claims that the bishops take the place of the apostles (1 Timothy 4:14), that it follows the order of the early Roman Government and also adapts the natural human tendency for organization.

Presbyterian: In this the local Church is governed by a group of elders and the denomination is governed by elected representatives of local Churches (1 Timothy 5:17).

Reasons for this include that it provides a check on a pastor, copies most of what we know of New Testament time practice (copying the Jewish methods of the day (Luke 7:3), that it tries to make sure that no one person dominates the local Church and that the inter Church aspect (in a presbytery) provides a check on any one Church.

Hallmarks of the Church

Jesus when praying in John 17:17-21 stipulates these four hallmarks of His Church: one (John 17:21), holy (John 17:17, 19), catholic (John 17:21) and apostolic (John 17:18). These hallmarks show how the Spirit will continue the witness to, and work of, Jesus in His kingdom, and are the true Church's indisputable marks. The term 'one holy, catholic and apostolic Church' is a verbal confession, denoting the four visible dimensions of the invisible Church as a community springing forth from its first century founding, and this is what was meant by the Nicene Creed, where the phrase was first agreed (at a great meeting of all the then Churches held in AD 381). The Church evolves from generation to generation but should never lose the core beliefs stated in the Nicene Creed. Catholic here, in case anyone requires clarification, means universal and not the denomination.

While these four hallmarks are statements of faith, they also must lead to declarations of function, because the Church must be actively visible. The four derived functions of the Church are: fellowship, worship, mission and bible interaction. We will look at each of these later in this book. They are mutually interdependent and are the invisible Church's visible expressions.

1.2. The Church Is One

"I will remain in the world no longer, but they are still in the world, and I am coming to you. Holy Father, protect them by the power of your name, the name you gave me, so that they may be one as we are one." (John 17:11)

From this verse of Scripture, we see that Jesus prayed to the Father that His body the Church would be involved in a united and dynamic relationship (John 17:11). By the way, when referring to Church here, I am speaking of the one universal and invisible Church, and not the local visible Churches.

There can only be one Church, because there is only one Saviour, Jesus Christ and therefore, only one body within which salvation can be found. It is unique, and the whole Church is Jesus Christ's Bride, Body and Temple. There is only one Christ, therefore there can only be one Church, the body of Christ. The unifying fellowship people have with each other is founded only upon Jesus. There was only one Cross, therefore there can only be one Kingdom and one Church. There is only one God, therefore there could only be one people and one Church known by its unity (Ephesians 4:4-6). Jesus stipulated that there is one shepherd and one flock, when referring to Himself and His followers the Church (John 10:16, the other sheep are the non-Jewish believers that were to come).

Unity however does not mean uniformity. Provided core beliefs are maintained (1 Corinthians 15:3-4), there appears to be room for some 'things indifferent' where there can be, and even should be, different views regarding secondary beliefs (Romans 14:1–15:13). Individual Churches have different local needs to be faced, and therefore have dissimilar requirements. For a group to claim that they alone have the ultimate truth and are the only true Church is the common behaviour of heretical cults and sects.

The **Biological** approach takes the view that the historical Church develops and evolves like tree branches.

The **Eschatological** viewpoint follows Calvin's theory of the invisible Church becoming visible and known only when revealed at the last day and only then will all present disunity be abolished.

The **Imperialist** view is favoured by the Roman Catholic Church, which claims that it is the only one Church that can be observed as having unity, thereby signifying its claim to be the one true Church.

The **Platonic view** claims that there is a basic distinction between the historical Church and the ideal Church.

The **Self-evident** view is revealed in the clear evidence from the differing worship styles of the New Testament Church. While most persevered with a Jewish worship model, others followed a different format (1 Corinthians 14:26-40). To further illustrate the problem faced by having one universal Church yet a multitude of visible local Churches, there are four distinct approaches which help explain this tension: imperialist, Platonic, eschatological and biological.

However, the saying of Ignatius, an early Father of the Church, *"ubi Christus, ibi ecclesia"* implies very strongly that the Church's unity is found only in Christ.[1] The united Church is a spiritual entity, not to be judged by external signs and values but to be founded only upon God's unity within the Trinitarian Godhead.

As for the sacraments, the Eucharist, is to be celebrated together in fellowship with other believers, hence its name

---

[1] Translated as "Where Christ is, there is the Church"

in some traditions as Holy Communion. Baptism is also done with others as an act of fellowship, with others performing the baptism and acting as witnesses. This hallmark, the quality of 'One', can be tested in any Church and is revealed in the function of fellowship. The test of this hallmark in any Church is the extent to which it requires fellowship If fellowship exists and is functioning, then the Church can be seen to be participating in this hallmark and be 'one'.

Function: Fellowship

One aspect of the Church being 'one' is that its members have fellowship, resulting from walking with one another (1 John 1:7). The Church is a gathering of humans, engaging in human activities with human "customs, texts, orders, procedures and possessions" through the power of the Holy Spirit.

What is fellowship? This is rooted in the Greek words koinōnia and koinōneō, which is defined as a mutual sharing together, and not merely a mutual association. The New Testament Church understood the word both in having fellowship and giving fellowship.

Why fellowship? When Christian Disciples fellowship with each other, God is glorified as a result (Romans 15:7). It is as a collective body that the Church fellowship grows in grace and maturity together, overcoming by grace, the weaknesses of each individual member (Ephesians 4:12-16).

Another reason for fellowship is for mutual exhortation "toward love and good deeds" (Hebrews 10:25). By participating actively in fellowship, individual Church members can live a consistent godly life, particularly if sins are confessed to each other (James 5:16). New Testament exhortations to live holy lives are said to groups (Romans 6:1-23) and victory is also seen in the eyes of a fellowship or community, rather than singular individuals (1 Corinthians

15:57; 1 John 4:11; 5:4). Whilst God deals with us as individuals, it is through fellowship that God strengthens the individual, for individuals are "complemented, supported, healed and compensated" by other Christians. These are all very good reasons why all Christian Disciples need to find a Church to attend!

How do we fellowship? Biblical fellowship sees the Church having common purpose (Psalm 133:1-3), belief (Acts 2:42), hope (Hebrews 11:39-40) and needs (2 Corinthians 8:1-15). Just as Christians have fellowship with the Father (1 John 1:3), Jesus (1 Corinthians 1:9) and the Holy Spirit (Philippians 2:1), so do they have with each other (1 John 1:7).

The things a fellowship shares in, yet not limited to, are possessions (2 Corinthians 8:4), sufferings (Philippians 3:10) and the Gospel (Galatians 2:9; Philippians 1:5). Paul tells us that through his own sufferings, he was participating in Jesus' suffering and was having fellowship with Jesus. Therefore, Paul was able to enter into an ever deeper and intimate relationship with Jesus.

1.3. The Church Is Holy

[17] Sanctify them by the truth; your word is truth. [18] As you sent me into the world, I have sent them into the world. [19] For them I sanctify myself, that they too may be truly sanctified. (John 17:17-19)

From these verses of Scripture, we see that Jesus prayed to the Father that His body, the Church, would be holy! There are 2 different words in English, sounding very different, but meaning the same thing "holy" and "sanctify". We tend to think of "holy" as a state and "sanctify" as the process by which we can become holy.

Yet we must ask, how is the Church made holy? The Church is made holy through Jesus' holy sacrifice on the cross and the Holy Spirit's sanctifying work within individual believers (1 Corinthians 6:11).

The Church is holy, in that it is God's separated people living in the community, in the power of the Holy Spirit, and through a perfecting faith in Jesus Christ (2 Corinthians 7:1). The Church is not to be an exclusive and holy society secluded from the world, but rather God's salvation bearing movement going out to the world.

Jesus Christ is the head of the Church, and therefore the quality of a Church's relationship with Him, is identified through biblical morality and faithfulness to His teaching. When in the book of Revelation, Jesus did not find holiness in the Churches he condemned them (Revelation 2:20-23), but continued to call them His bride. Augustine (another early Church Father) cites Christ's holiness as the reason for the Church' present holiness and how the Church will be made perfect on the last day.

However, being holy does not just mean being sinless. Holiness also means to be separated out and set apart for

God's special purpose and work. This work is to spread the Gospel to all parts of the earth; the task of His chosen people, the Church - people who are, and were, being sanctified by the Holy Spirit and rooted in Gospel truth (2 Thessalonians 2:13-14).

Wherever the Bible is preached faithfully, the Church consisting of God's holy people also resides. However, it should be noted that in addition to this, the Church also requires those who are truly saved = those who have accepted Jesus' free offer of salvation and in relationship with God. The method by which this hallmark can be tested in any Church can be observed in the function of worship. If the community is a worshipping community, then the Church can be seen to be 'holy'.

Function: Worship

Worship as a Church function derives from the hallmark of the Church being holy. Worship is an intimate, dynamic and holy encounter with God, because Jesus is in the midst (Matthew 18:20) and empowered by the Holy Spirit (Philippians 3:3).

What is worship? Worship is giving God alone the glory due His name in the beauty of His holiness (1 Chronicles 16:29). The prime element of worshipping God in the context of a Church is reverence. This is where through the willing use of the mind and the senses, honour and respect are directed towards God. This is to be done "in the Spirit and in truth" (John 4:24). The word 'spirit' here, denotes the personal status of worship involving the entire person – mind, body and will, all interacting in connection to the indwelling Holy Spirit. Truth speaks of worship's content, in that all true worship certainly reflects God's character and majesty. Worship therefore is multiform in practice, with richness in the breadth of its distinctive styles, to the one God deserving of all that we are and have. The Christian Church has 2000 years of worship resources, all of which can be used in modern Church services, and not just the songs from the last 2 years. Why are people to worship? There are various reasons as to why the Church worships God, although primarily because God commands it.

> Ascribe to the Lord the glory due His name; bring an offering and come before him. Worship the Lord in the splendour of His holiness. (1 Chronicles 16:29)

The Ten Commandments, also known as the Decalogue, also clearly command people to worship God alone (Exodus 20:3-10). Not only is it a command, but God deserves worshipping by His Church for He alone personifies goodness (Psalm 100:4-5), mercy (Exodus 4:31), holiness (Psalm 99:5, 9) and power (Revelation 4:11).

God is to be worshipped by His Church in obedience to Him as the great Creator (Revelation 4:11) but also as its Saviour and Lord (Habakkuk 3:18). Worship also is to bring exuberant satisfaction upon the worshipper (Romans 12:2; Colossians 3:24). How can this worship be expressed? Scripture speaks of various means by which the Church worships God, including joyful singing (Psalm 100:2; Ephesians 5:19) and public declarations of praise. The writer to the Hebrews states:

> Through Jesus, therefore, let us continually offer to God a sacrifice of praise – the fruit of lips that openly profess his name. (Hebrews 13:15)

Perhaps the greatest manifestation of public Church worship is seen when Christians gather to participate in the sacraments. The Protestant Church has two ordinances, or sacraments.

Holy Communion: Celebrating Holy Communion is in direct obedience of Jesus' command that all Christian

Disciples are to celebrate the remembrance of Him (Matthew 26:26-28; Luke 22:19-20). Partaking in Holy Communion not only symbolizes His death for our sin (Luke 22:19), but also symbolizes the Christian Disciple's acceptance of Christ's death for them and their dependence on Him for spiritual life (John 6:35).

Baptism: Baptism is commanded for all Christian Disciples (Matthew 28:19; Acts 2:38), and quite naturally follows on after conversion to Christ (Acts 2:37). To be baptized means to be baptized into Christ (Romans 6:3), which symbolizes a total identification with Jesus because of being baptized into His body (1 Corinthians. 12:13) and into His death (Romans 6:1-6). Through baptism, the Christian Disciples' sinful nature is seen as dead with Christ (Romans 6:6), and we are raised to live a new life with a new nature (Romans 6:4)! Isn't that an amazing result of God's amazing grace and mercy towards us?

1.4. The Church Is Catholic

[20] 'My prayer is not for them alone. I pray also for those who will believe in me through their message, [21] that all of them may be one, Father, just as you are in me and I am in you. May they also be in us so that the world may believe that you have sent me. (John 17:20-21)

The word 'catholic' derives from the Greek word '*katholios*', and its first written appearance is in Ignatius' Epistle to the Smyrnaeans. Second century Christians used it to describe themselves, signifying that God's salvific truth was to be communicated across the world, transcending all barriers of nationality, culture and language.

The word was also used to symbolize their distinction from the heretics and their false teachings. In the mandate of what we call 'the Great Commission', Jesus commands that the Gospel is spread throughout the world, and the Church was to be His witnesses empowered by the Holy Spirit.[2]

Whilst the other first century religions were exclusivist by race, intellect or other means, Christianity was unique in that it was open for all, regardless of gender, race, culture or class. Paul had this in mind when he wrote There is neither Jew nor Gentile, neither slave nor free, nor is there male and female, for you are all one in Christ Jesus" (Galatians 3:28). The Gospel message proclaimed was for all people everywhere, including those with immoral pasts.

While the word 'catholic' may be defined as 'universal', it can also be understood as referring to the whole. This is because a 'catholic Church' is a whole Church, in so much

---

[2] Matthew 28:18-20

as because the Gospel impacts every aspect of a human and the 'catholic' Church addresses the heart, mind and will of all people everywhere.

The Church possesses, within itself, every kind of virtue which can be named and has complete access to words, deeds or spiritual gifts of every kind. It is also whole or universal in its relation to time and history; in so much as there has always been a people of God and will remain so until and after the end of time on earth. It is participation within the Church of the past, the present Church and Church of the future, which reflects catholicity.

It is through the function of mission that this hallmark can be tested in any Church and can be discerned in the Church. If, in conjunction with the other hallmarks, the Church community engages in gospel outreach, then the Church can be seen to be 'catholic'.

Function: Mission

The Church's mission is evangelism – proclaiming the good news from God about Jesus Christ. This is sourced from the Church being marked as catholic. Evangelism is the virtue of bringing God's reconciling message of salvation to all people of all time in all places without barrier or hindrance. Throughout the Book of Acts, we see the commitment to mission in practice, as God's reconciling message spread through His Church to Jerusalem, Judea, Samaria and into the Gentile lands. This was in response to Jesus' words:

> [7] He said to them: 'It is not for you to know the times or dates the Father has set by his own authority.
> [8] But you will receive power when the Holy Spirit comes on you; and you will be my witnesses in Jerusalem, and in all Judea and Samaria, and to the ends of the earth.'
> (Acts 1:7-8)

What is evangelism? Evangelism is telling God's message of reconciliation to all people of all time. It is not forcing people to adopt Church standards (1 Corinthians 5:12); nor is it simply a message of joining the Church as a symbol of good works (Ephesians 2:8-10). This catholic, or universal, gospel says that everybody has sinned against God (Isaiah 53:6; Romans 3:10-11); that nobody can earn their own reconciliation with God (Ephesians 2:9); that God sent His Son Jesus to be born, crucified and resurrected so that salvation can be had for all people of all time (John 3:16; 1 Timothy 1:15). People are saved by submitting themselves to God by faith in Jesus alone (John 5:24; Acts 16:31).

Why are Christians to evangelize? The prime motivation for evangelism is out of gratitude for what God has done for the individual and the Church, in that we love God, simply because He loved us first (1 John 4:10-12, 14 & 19). It was with this sentiment Paul refers to when he writes:

"For Christ's love compels us, because we are convinced that one died for all, and therefore all died." (2 Corinthians 5:14).

The New Testament Church told of God's reconciling message out of an "overwhelming experience of God's love" which they had received. Also, God is a missionary God. Jesus was sent to save the lost and redeem mankind! The Holy Spirit was sent from the Father and the Son for the same purpose!

While some are explicitly called to be evangelists (Ephesians 4:11), it also falls on all members of the Church to do the work of an evangelist, following the example of Timothy (2 Timothy 4:5). Scripture dictates several reasons for members of His Church to share their faith. Jesus commands us to tell others of God's reconciling message. In the last words of Jesus' earthly ministry, His Church was commanded to be witnesses for Him (Acts 1:8). Evangelism is also an expression of the Christian Disciple's love for God, through obeying His commands (John 14:15) and their love of other people and wanting others to be in God's Kingdom. It is also the Church's imperative mission because the Church is the vessel God has chosen to spread the message of reconciliation to all people and of all time (Acts 4:12; 2 Peter 3:9). That includes you, if you are a Christian today. The Apostle Paul elucidates upon this to the Roman Church:

"How, then, can they call on the one they have not believed in? And how can they believe in the one of whom they have not heard? And how can they hear without someone preaching to them? And how can they preach unless they are sent? As it is written, "How beautiful are the feet of those who bring good news!" (Romans 10:14-15)

What is Evangelism?

[1] And so it was with me, brothers and sisters. When I came to you, I did not come with eloquence or human wisdom as I proclaimed to you the testimony about God. [2] For I resolved to know nothing while I was with you except Jesus Christ and him crucified. [3] I came to you in weakness with great fear and trembling. [4] My message and my preaching were not with wise and persuasive words, but with a demonstration of the Spirit's power, [5] so that your faith might not rest on human wisdom, but on God's power. (1 Corinthians 2:1-5)

While Paul was going the 50 miles or so from Athens to Corinth, he was alone. He had left the intellectual centre of the ancient world, Athens, and entered Corinth, the cultural capital of the ancient world. Do you sometimes think that

Paul resembled a superman, always brash and utterly confident when engaged in evangelism? According to this passage, he entered with great nervousness, weakness and fear. He was not confident in His own ability or the way that he spoke and reasoned. But why should Paul have been this way in the city of Corinth?

Paul in Corinth

The city of Corinth is located on the narrow isthmus linking northern and southern Greece. It had two ports, one on either side, from which small ships and boats could be dragged on greased planks the 3-mile journey across the isthmus, thus saving themselves a 200-mile journey through dangerous waters right round southern Greece. It was therefore a natural place for fantastic links for commerce and culture across the known world. The world famous Isthmian games were held there.

Paul's reasoning for deciding to go there was probably along the lines of "If it is good enough for commerce and culture to be spread from Corinth, even better for the Gospel to travel far and wide from that hub." So, he enters Corinth. But alas, with culture and commerce came its evil triplet – immorality.

The temple, which overlooked Corinth, was dedicated to the goddess Aphrodite and had 1,000 prostitutes. Aphrodite was the goddess of love and sex. In those days to go "corinthianizing", meant to go actively seeking immorality. These are the reasons why Paul entered Corinth nervously. The city was known for its proud and cultural intelligentsia, endemic immorality and there were many temples to many deities. The Corinthians were post-modern people, long before post-modernity. Their motto – "If it feels good, do it." Paul was nervous and weak in His own strength, but he was supremely confident in the Lord and the power of the Spirit to use him. What can we learn from Paul's visit to Corinth and how do we apply that to our lives today in the 21st century? After all our modern cities and towns are not very different from ancient Corinth.

Wherever he travelled, Paul's message was the Gospel which proclaims that "Jesus is Lord" (Romans 10:9) This was decidedly dangerous as it was a direct challenge to the Roman Empire who taught that "Caesar is Lord".

The Gospel is Trinitarian in that it is the Father's mysterious revelation through the Son's work on the cross in the power of the Spirit. The Gospel is also three-dimensional in that it covers the breadth of the Bible – all of Scripture is about God's plan of Salvation; the depth of the cross of Jesus Christ and the length of God's mission. The Gospel was, and is, anathema and unpopular to those outside of the Kingdom of God. Just as it was a direct challenge to the ancient Roman Empire, so it is today. The Gospel is never popular, and if it is, then it is not a truly Biblical Gospel.

For instance, some Churches proclaim a false Gospel where financial & health prosperity is the central claim. We have a false Gospel where Jesus is a cure-all being the central claim. We've a false Gospel wherever it is used for political purposes. For Paul, and for all true Christian Disciples the true Gospel is this: "Jesus and Him crucified" (1 Corinthians 2:2).

Paul faced Jewish opposition, in that to the Jewish mind-set, it was unthinkable that their Messiah would be crucified on a pagan Gentile cross (Acts 18:6, 12-17). Paul also faced Gentile opposition - Paul's claim that "Jesus is Lord of all" was a direct and dangerous challenge to the prevailing idea throughout the empire that Caesar was the 'Lord of all'.

For example, opposition from the Corinthians. Jesus' exclusive claim to be the only way, the only truth and the only life challenged Corinthian pluralism & universalism. The Corinthian people lived a life filled with many gods, why would they want to settle for just the One God – particularly one who had died? A life of holiness challenged Corinthian immorality. God's power challenged Corinthian cultured intellect. When Paul was in Athens, some Athenians told Paul he was a babbler. A sentiment undoubtedly echoed by the cultured and refined Corinthian intelligentsia.

Humility would have also challenged Corinthian pride. To kneel at the cross, takes great humility. The action of doing so as exhibited and proclaimed by Paul, would have caused derision and his words classed as talked complete and utter nonsense. The Corinthian people were proud and cultured, and as such, to whom the very thought of humbly kneeling before any God, was at best, to be seen as unadulterated anathema. For the Corinthians, it was much better to be seen to be devoting yourself to one of the goddesses of sex. What more could a young Corinthian want than the mixture of religion and sex?

Evangelism Today

The same applies today. We are shouted down if we dare exclaim that Jesus is Lord and the only acceptable path to God. That is particularly the case if you live in a country which worships other gods or is under tight control of those who do not believe in any god. In the West, we are told Jesus Christ is not significant at all, if He even existed at all outside of ancient fairy tales akin to 'Chinese whispers'. We are told that universal moral absolutes do not exist, and that what's right for you may not be right for me and providing I am not hurting anyone, stay out of my private business. Sex and sexuality are worshipped and adored as if they were gods in themselves. We live in an age of Scientific

Materialism and hyper-rationalism, where people cynically laugh at us and say that at best, Christians worship a dead man. We are often called fools for believing in a God. Have you had those things said to you? I know that I have been in the past, and no doubt, I shall be again in the future.

Humility is not looked upon as a strength today, it is frowned upon as a weakness. The world says that if you want to get ahead in life, you need to be strong, show some backbone and don't ever back down to anybody or anything. Certainly, as a 21st century person, you should never admit you were wrong and had made mistakes. That is counter to the Gospel, which insists that the way of Jesus Christ, is to kneel before the Cross, admit your mistakes and sins and be prepared to serve and take up your own cross and that is directly antagonistic to the culture.

The world is quite willing to accept a harmless baby at Christmas, but not the violence of the cross that followed. That is why even atheists sing Christmas Carols. The danger of Christmas is when the gloriously unique incarnation of Jesus Christ, being both fully God and fully human, is diluted into fantasy along with Santa Claus and His elves. All Christian Disciples are called to do the work of evangelism. Not everyone is called to be an evangelist, like Billy Graham, yet all Christians are indeed called to tell and show others about their Master, Jesus Christ. That is what evangelism is. Consider the following statement made by Paul to his young charge, Timothy.

5 "But you, keep your head in all situations, endure hardship, do the work of an evangelist, discharge all the duties of your ministry." (2 Timothy 4:5)

The approach to evangelism has changed over the last few years. As Christian Disciples, it is the job of all Christian Disciples to evangelise and witness about Jesus, using the skills and perceptions they inherently hold. We are not to leave it up the Billy Graham's and Luis Palau's of this world. There isn't just one style of evangelism to be employed. Interpersonal, invitational, serving, testimonial, intellectual or confrontational styles are available for Churches and Christian Disciples to use. A Christian Disciple's use of any or all these styles would be dependent on their own personality, talents and skills. However, you do it or whoever you are, sharing the Gospel is for all Christian Disciples.

Innovative evangelism

Not only would this make it new for the congregation, but add an element of excitement, particularly if old evangelistic methods are being employed, and seemingly ineffective. Some ideas such as, having a prayer stall at the local market, or taking over a vacant shop on the high street for the explicit purpose of praying for people. The Church could offer the use of its website as a local community forum, or 'virtual local community hall, for community notices.

Another way would be to hold internet-based events and/or forums, so that those who are housebound or are part of what some call the Internet Generation, have a platform to converse and discover about Christianity, for their youth and student work. Rightly or wrongly, the truth is that people are gathering like that, and discussing Christian issues. New methods can also be seen as making use of every opportunity.

Early starters

New believers are often encouraged to evangelise from the time of their conversion. That utilises the first flush of enthusiasm and makes it seem that there is not a two-step process of conversion and then later undergoing evangelism training. It makes use of the fact that they gained perceptions about evangelism, whilst they were being evangelised. Evangelism is to be what a Christian Disciple is, rather than merely an activity that a Christian Disciple engages in.

Lead by teaching

As evangelism is prayed about, activated, discussed and enacted, Christian Disciples undergo evangelism training, even if they aren't aware of it at the time. A good method is for training to be given, not just as a one-off exercise but throughout the year.

The reason for this is so that every member has an opportunity to undergo some formal training when it is convenient for them as they see the leadership committed to evangelistic training. This training should be promoted by the Church leadership from the front of the Church, so that every member can see the seriousness with which the leadership think about evangelism. Evangelism is key to the growth of the Church and is an obedient response to Jesus Christ who is the Lord and Master of the Church (Matthew 28:18-20).

Lead by example

We see throughout the New Testament narrative, that Church leaders led by example, and actively persuaded others to do as they did. Paul certainly commanded that the Corinthian Church follow him as he imitated Jesus Christ (1 Corinthians 11:1). This is a model full of dynamism. Others can go on doing the work in their own way, without relying upon the Church leaders. Does your Church work like that in any way?

Remember

The main lesson for Christian Disciples to learn, is that evangelism can only be truly effective when undertaken under an umbrella of prayer and the work of the Holy Spirit. It is the Holy Spirit's power and authority, which allows the skills and talents of all people to be used as effective Gospel messengers. As Christian Disciples we need to continually remind ourselves that it is Jesus Christ who is building the Church, and that with the Holy Spirit's power, we are neither alone nor powerless. After all, He is a Holy Spirit of evangelism.

That is why as Christian Disciples, we need not fear the supposed rise of fundamental atheism or any other religion or – "ism". We have the power of the Living God within us, to equip and use us for His glory and mission. People may be able to remove the supposed 'spirit of Christmas' from schools and other government buildings, but they can never take away the Spirit of Christ that indwells all Christian disciples.

When in Corinth, despite His nervousness and worries, Paul knew God was in control (Acts 18:10) and that's why he stayed a further 18 months following His vision where God promised protection, security, companionship and success (Acts 18:11). Paul endured in the face of opposition (Acts 18:12-16). Here we read that the Jewish leaders went to the Roman proconsul Gallio, complaining that Paul had started a new religion, for starting a new religion was forbidden under Roman law. Anything that was a religion before the Romans took control, such as Judaism, was seen as a legitimate religion. Gallio however dismissed the Jewish case as mere internal bickering about minor details and dismissed the complaint. In doing so, Gallio made Christianity a legitimate religion within the Roman Empire, and that is probably why Paul stayed in Corinth a good deal

God, Internet Church & You

longer (Acts 18:18). Paul did not succumb to the temptations around him, because he only sought one thing – to declare "Jesus Christ and Him crucified" (1 Corinthians 2:2).

The world around likes to play clever tricks on us, just as the Jewish leadership did with Paul. But we are to be, as Jesus commanded "shrewd as snakes and as innocent as doves." (Matthew 10:16). We are to stay faithful to Jesus despite difficulties. It means staying faithful to Him, regardless of opposition and attractive alternatives. By doing this we endure and remain faithful.

Overcoming barriers

There are at least seven reasons why Christian Disciples choose not to evangelise others. Christian Disciples who overcome these hindrances, are then liberated to share the Gospel with others, not least, locally.
Barriers can be overcome, but first we need to know what those barriers are and what these barriers consist of
- Thinking others will wonder what took you so long, if you evangelise them now
- Do not know the Bible well enough to answer questions
- Entire friends are already Christian Disciples
- Testimony is perceived to be dull and tedious
- Don't know if my friends are true Christian Disciples or not
- There is no easy way to tell the Gospel
- Basic shyness in talking to strangers

Method & Message

The early Church preached that God, who is outside of both time and space, entered human time and history as a

36

human baby. This baby was Jesus, and His purpose was "to give His life as a ransom for many." (Mark 10:45) The early Church grew expansively because of the early Church taking the message of Jesus seriously and under persecution from others. But what clues and tips can we take from them to help us today? We can see these by looking at the pioneer of urban mission, the man we know as the Apostle Paul. After all, it is from His letters and writings we can gain a glimpse into this early Church pioneer.

Paul's Places

We start by looking at where Paul evangelized and shared the message of salvation. Paul evangelised wherever it was that people gathered together: whether Paul was in the Synagogue (Acts 18:4-6), in the marketplace or at a place of work (Acts 18:3, 13). Paul certainly had His fears, frustrations and limitations of His own weaknesses, as a cursory look at His letters show us, but he managed to overcome them and learnt to rely totally on God's power. Much of the early church was the same. For us today, the same can indeed be equally true.

Paul's Method

If that is where Paul shared the message, what about the various methods that we read he employed as he ventured through the known world? Paul reasoned from the Scriptures (Acts 18:3-4, 11), knowing that Scripture had been revealed, inspired and illuminated by God. Paul knew Scripture equipped people for service of God, helping them to know God more intimately. Paul recognized that Scripture revealed God's programme for the world and that getting to know Scripture was vital in order to be used in

Evangelism. In doing so, Paul was prepared to change strategy (Acts 18:6), invited people home and that he was careful to forge relationships (Acts 18:2, 6-8, 17). How is our method of Evangelism in the Church today, to be similar to that of the Apostle Paul?

The Gospel Message

Central to the Gospel, the Good News of God to humanity, is the Cross. A question we need to ask is why is the Cross so central to the Gospel? Paul's Gospel message was "Jesus and Him crucified" (1 Corinthians 2:2). The Gospel is Jesus and that is why that proclamation is central to the Gospel message.

As important as the incarnation, resurrection and ascension are, the Gospel is Jesus Christ. Not just a Jesus to whom anything can be attached. Ideas such as being a good friend, but the Jesus who was the God-man, who lived in this world, was falsely accused, condemned, crucified, rose again and ascended into heaven. In other words the whole story of His life and death, and not just picking choosing selected parts which take the fancy of the individual. At the very centre of that story, and most significant for us, was that Jesus' death secured salvation for all who follow Him, and it was His resurrection which proved that He was the Messiah, that He said He was.

Without Jesus' death on the cross there would be no Christianity, and consequently no hope for the world. Therefore, the interpretation that we place on Jesus' death is of first importance. That He died is without doubt, but why did He have to die and what gain do we have as His Disciples? By His very nature, God is loving and compassionate, forgiving, faithful and slow to anger (Exodus 34:6-7). This is the part, if we are being honest, all of us are most comfortable with. Yet God is holy, righteous and just and must punish sin because of this very same nature. That is the part which we as 21st century people are uncomfortable with, if we are being honest. We like to think of God as being all love and gentleness, but don't like to think of Him as a Judge who must punish disobedience. But we also need to remember that God loves righteousness and hates wickedness (Psalm 45:7).

Therefore wickedness, that is sin & disobedience must be dealt with and it cannot simply be ignored. Regardless of how much we would like God to do just that. Sin is humanity's problem. It is part of our problem as humans. A quick observation around us in the media, will show that to be self-apparent.

The Problem - Humanity's sin

Sin is what separates humans from God and as a consequence leads them to both a spiritual and physical death (Isaiah 59:2, Romans 6:23). Nobody escapes as all have sinned and fallen short of the glory of God (Romans 3:23). In the Old Testament, sins were dealt with by blood sacrifices of atonement as coverings for sin (Leviticus 17:11), for without the shedding of blood there can be no forgiveness (Hebrews 9:22).

The Solution – God to the rescue

The solution lies not in the continual animal sacrifices of the Old Testament because Hebrews 10:4 reminds us that the blood of animals cannot take away sin but was only a veneer or covering. That was why it was necessary to repeat time and time again. It is only through the death of Jesus, that sin is taken away (Hebrews 9:11-15, 26-28), and that was only needed once, because Jesus was God and His death was all powerful. Therefore, Jesus is our permanent sacrificial substitute. That is why the elements of bread and wine in Communion or Breaking of Bread are symbolic, and not somehow changed into actual flesh and blood, as some would have us believe. There is no possibility of a repetition of the Cross.

Substitution

> For Christ also suffered once for sins, the righteous for the unrighteous, to bring you to God. He was put to death in the body but made alive in the Spirit. (1 Peter 3:18)

Jesus died for our sin, the righteous for the unrighteous (1 Peter 3:18). That is how God can be both just and the Justifier (another way of saying righteous and the 'righteous-ifier', (Romans 3:26)) of sinners and that is why Jesus needed to be both fully God and fully human. If he lacked either, it would not be the full substitutionary sacrifice that was necessary to bear the permanent consequences of sin. This substitution was the sacrifice required in order that Jesus as the Lamb of God could take away the sins of the world (John 1:29). He was the propitiation, the necessary cover, for all sin.

Propitiation

The word 'propitiation' is a difficult word for our modern English language, that some of the modern Bible translations do not use it. Yes, it can raise all sorts of awkward questions. As well as using this word, which is in the original manuscripts, I will give an alternate word. Some people use it in their teaching and some people do not. That way you can make up your own mind regarding it. Propitiation is the turning aside of God's anger by the offering of the sacrifice of Christ. Towards sin and sinful behaviour God necessarily has great fury, anger and wrath (Jeremiah 21:5). Hebrews 10:30-31 reminds us, "It is dreadful to fall into the hands of the living God." Yet as Micah 7:18 "He is slow to anger and quick to forgive". God's anger and judgment of sin falls on Christ, instead of us. We need to approach God to appease His anger, in order to accept it (Romans 3:25; Isaiah 53:5; John 2:2, John 5:6).

Reconciliation

Our other word used instead of propitiation is reconciliation. We need to be reconciled to God, that is to become friends with God, to become 'at one with God', hence '*at-one-ment*'. God has been justly angry with us because of our sinfulness and failure to recognize him as God. This reconciliation is accomplished by the turning aside of God's anger through the offering of the sacrifice of Christ, what is called the 'sacrifice of atonement' in Romans 3:25.

Towards sin and sinful behaviour God necessarily has great fury, anger and wrath (Jeremiah 21:5). Yet, as the writer to the Hebrews reminds us:

"It is a dreadful thing to fall into the hands of the living God." (Hebrews 10:30-31)

However, the prophet Micah also reminds us that:

Yet as says "He pardons sin and forgives the transgression". (Micah 7:18)

God's anger and judgment of sin falls on Christ, instead of us. We need to approach God in faith to accept what Christ did on the Cross, to receive His gracious present, and so to have His anger turned aside from us (Romans 3:25; Isaiah 53:5; John 2:5, John 5:6). To some people, even some in the

Church, this is abhorrent. The very thought that God could willing send His son to be a blood sacrifice for sin is tantamount to child abuse and God would therefore be the cosmic child-abuser. Some people think Jesus' crucifixion was an act of sado-masochism. Neither of these opinions are valid or true. Nor can they ever be. God's requirements are very clear in response to this, as we have briefly seen together. If there were another way, then surely God would have done it that way.

"For God so loved the world, that He gave His one and only Son that whoever believes in Him shall not perish but have eternal life". (John 3:16)

Redemption

Not only was it propitiation (a sacrifice of atonement which accomplished reconciliation), but it is also an act of redemption. In the time of the New Testament, this word redemption was used to refer to the buying back of a slave - the price paid to buy the slave's freedom. In Christian thinking, God paid redemption so that humans could choose to be freed from the slavery to sin (John 8:35; Romans 6:22, Romans 7:14; Titus 2:14). The price was paid with the precious blood of God the Son, Jesus Christ (1 Peter 1:18-19) and so we are bought at that high price (1 Corinthians 6:19-20).

As Christian Disciples, we have a new position before God. We are bought out of slavery to sin, into the glorious freedom where we are now slaves to righteousness (Romans 6:19) and slaves of God (Romans 6:22). All those who are truly Christian disciples are also Jesus Christ's personal possession: But it is our responsibility to choose that way. God does not force us to love him – He leaves it as a choice for humans to make as individuals.

But you are a chosen people, a royal priesthood, a

holy nation, God's special possession, that you may declare the praises of him who called you out of darkness into His wonderful light. (1 Peter 2:9)

Our response?

What is our response to all this to be? Sacrifice, substitution, propitiation, reconciliation and redemption can be summed up in one word: love.

Jesus commanded that all those who would follow Him, were to take up their cross if they were to follow Him as His Disciple (Luke 9:23). Are you as a Christian Disciple willing to take up your cross and do all you can do to follow him and love others – all other people?

"This is how we know what love is: Jesus Christ laid down His life for us. And we ought to lay down our lives for our brothers and sisters." (1 John 3:16)

Testimony

A testimony is an assertion offering first-hand authentication of a fact. For the Christian Disciple, classically it is generally expressed as how they became a Christian Disciple. But I think it should be more than just about that initial step and should expressly include why you are a Christian Disciple, and what that means to you now. Here is how the Apostle John describes them.

[9] We accept human testimony, but God's testimony is greater because it is the testimony of God, which he has given about His Son. [10] Whoever believes in the Son of God accepts this testimony. Whoever does not believe God has made him out to be a liar, because they have not believed the testimony God has given about His Son. [11] And this is the testimony: God has given us eternal life, and this life is in His

Son. [12] Whoever has the Son has life; whoever does not have the Son of God does not have life. (1 John 5:9-12)

Why Is It So?

What is your testimony about how you became a Christian Disciple? When was the last time you thanked our God for your testimony? Have you even thought about your testimony of how you became a Christian Disciple? I am sure you have all heard kids in the supermarket yelling out "Why?" to their parents. We all have, I am sure, questions we want to know the answer to. Why? The question I am often asked is "You are a Christian. Why is it so?"

My father was and remained throughout His life, a convinced agnostic and in the few conversations we had about religion and Christianity, he could never understand why it was that I could not just admit that I would never know if God existed or not, far less a God who was personally interested in me. My reply as ever, was that the very question "Why is it so?" needed to be answered, in order for me to be satisfied. It is part of my story; just as similar stories are part of the life of other people.

Why I am a Christian?

Another question. Why am I a Christian? Now, I could say that at the age of 12 we moved to a town on the coast of Australia and was invited along to a local youth group and several weeks later, gave my life to Christ and became a Christian. Of course, that is partly true. I can't even claim to be a Christian because I was raised in a Christian country. Australia was, and is, one of the most secular countries on this planet. Sure, Australia has its moral base grounded in historic Christianity, but for the latter part of its history,

Australia has been thoroughly secular and non-religious. Even if I had been raised in a country such as England, technically Christian as it was, with Christian parents, I would not necessarily have become a Christian. I could have rejected Christianity as many people do.

The reason that I am a Christian is not because I chased God, but rather He chased me. Unknown to me at the time, God was chasing me and following my every path with the urgency of a lover after the beloved.

God in pursuit

This piece of poetic Scripture speaks about the love that God has for His people, and the energy He puts in to calling His people to Himself. He is always reaching out, seeking for all to return to His arms. As for me, it wasn't until I was a 12-year-old that I heard that I needed to accept Jesus as my Lord and Saviour. Before that I didn't know I had to do anything with this Jesus. Jesus was only a curse word for me at the time or was just someone or something that the Religious Education teachers bored me with at school.

If we are Christians, it is not because we attend Church services, or we just happened to have been born in a supposedly Christian country. It is entirely because God first chased and harried us into His arms. You are a Christian, if you are one, because God first loved you. And as a tremendous lover, He beckons and calls people all the time to respond to His call and turn back to Him. How does He chase us with His love?

He chases each person differently, just as each Christian testimony is different. Take for instance the Apostle Paul in Acts 8 and 9. God chased Paul through His mind and His religious upbringing and education. Paul had known about God from His childhood. Paul was a righteous Pharisee who thought persecuting these 'Christians' was His religious duty, so that he could demonstrate the strength of His devotion to God. As Paul was gloating over the death of the martyr Stephen, God was pursuing Him, probably raising doubts in Paul's mind as to why Stephen would say at the point of death "Lord Jesus, receive my spirit and forgive them for what they do" (Acts 7:54-60).

Surely doubts must have been raised in Paul's mind as he approved of this death (Acts 8:1). Paul was also wrestling with His conscience. Externally he was a righteous man, a Pharisee of Pharisees. Yet when he internally examined himself and His heart, he found himself failing regarding covetousness, which is the last of the Ten Commandments.

Then finally, Jesus himself makes a sudden and dramatic appearance before Paul and confronts him directly, "Saul, Saul, why do you persecute me?" (Acts 9:4)

Above all Paul suddenly discovered that Jesus was alive and well. What's more, this Jesus had risen from the dead! This led Paul to conclude that Jesus must be the Messiah. Paul's conversion to Christianity is often described as being sudden. But the only thing truly sudden about His conversion was this climactic appearance of Jesus.

Just as that was true of Paul, it is true of me, just as it is true of all those down through time, who profess to call themselves a Christian Disciple. I am a Christian Disciple not because of anything I have done, but rather because He first chased me, and because He first loved me. Jesus himself said:

"[10] For the Son of Man came to seek and to save the lost." (Luke 19:10).

If you are a Christian, it is not because of anything you have done. It is because of the events at Christmas and Easter that you are a Christian, when God entered this world as a human baby and took all the necessary steps so that all people could have the choice to be His people or not. In my more smug and prideful moments I used to congratulate myself for being a Christian. How proud I was that I was a Christian! It was with an attitude that God was a jolly lucky God that I had decided to follow Him. It was during one of my less self-deluded moments that I examined myself and I found God pricking my conscience and correcting me, and I read the New Testament God the Holy Spirit living within me, reminds me that it is by grace alone through faith alone, that I am a child of God – a child of the Living God. That is part of the message of Evangelism – people can choose to become children of God – Father, Son and Spirit – by God's grace through faith alone.

1.5. The Church Is Apostolic

As you sent me into the world, I have sent them into the world. (John 17:18)

There are two main reasons the Church is apostolic: apostolic mission and apostolic teaching. There is also a theory regarding the apostle Peter and papal succession. The two New Testament words translated as 'Apostle' are *'apostolos'* and *'apostolē'*, both of which signify mission and being sent out. Mission is at the heart of the apostolic Church in that it is sent into the world with a Gospel that is for all.

There are therefore, two assured reasons that the Church is apostolic. Firstly, the Church is founded on the authority of Apostle-based teaching as found in the New Testament and commanded by the apostolic mission in the Great Commission given by Jesus before He ascended (Matthew 28:18-20). Secondly the Church is apostolic because the Church, according to Paul, is founded upon the teachings of the Apostles (Ephesians 2:20). The Apostles, as witnesses to the very life and teachings of Jesus, and their teachings, were the identification mark that was considered normal practice for the early Church. The Apostles still play a role in Church life today, in that the Church's teaching, authority, life and preaching is based upon the apostolic teachings found in the New Testament.

Unfortunately, there is also a complicated theory that the Church was founded on the Apostle Peter himself, and that the Church today has an apostolic link to him via papal succession. Consequently, some argue every bishop is only a bishop if he has been consecrated by another bishop and every minister of the Church must be ordained by a consecrated bishop. This creates a strong hierarchy with control over the whole Church. This is based on the thinking that the Apostle Peter was distinct from the other apostles in that Jesus always chose him first and that he spoke freely and independently from and for the other apostles. It is also based on the tradition of *'Cathedra Petri'*, that states that Peter alone had Episcopal authority, and that this is passed down through the Roman Catholic Church and its pope. This view is based on Peter's confession of Jesus being the Christ, and Jesus stating that the keys to paradise are for Peter alone. But there is no sign of this in all the story in the New Testament.

> [13] When Jesus came to the region of Caesarea Philippi, he asked His disciples, 'Who do people say the Son of Man is?'
> [14] They replied, 'Some say John the Baptist; others say Elijah; and still others, Jeremiah or one of the prophets.'
> [15] 'But what about you?' he asked. 'Who do you say I am?'
> [16] Simon Peter answered, 'You are the Messiah, the Son of the living God.'
> [17] Jesus replied, 'Blessed are you, Simon son of Jonah, for this was not revealed to you by flesh and blood, but by my Father in heaven. [18] And I tell you that you are Peter, and on this rock, I will build my Church, and the gates of Hades will not overcome it. [19] I will give you the keys of the kingdom of heaven; whatever you bind on earth will be bound in heaven, and whatever you loose on earth will be loosed in heaven.' (Matthew 16:13-19)

Therefore, this interpretation is erroneous and there are a multitude of objections to this theory. The principle objection being that all of Scripture warrants that the Church is founded on all of the apostles and all of their teaching, and not just on the Apostle Peter alone. This is the correct view and to read anything else into the pretext and context of this passage of Scripture, is therefore erroneous. The test concerning this hallmark in relation to any Church, is by monitoring their interaction with the Bible. If the Church is a community engaging in Bible teaching, then the Church can be seen to truly be 'apostolic'.

Function: Bible Interaction

The apostolic Church devoted itself to teaching from the Apostles (Acts 2:42). When the early Church realized it had to decide which written teachings it could accept as having God given authority etc. one of the tests given to manuscripts in order for it to be considered part of the New Testament canon was its link to the apostles.

Other tests included answering questions. Were they accepted as authentic and used by the Church? Were they in agreement with the doctrine handed down from the Apostles? Were they self-authenticating, in so much as that godly men and women could recognize God's Word.

What is the Bible?

The Bible is the Word of God and is the instrument of the Holy Spirit to bring people to faith (Ephesians 1:13) and ongoing sanctification (Ephesians 5:26). Paul writes that all of it is "God-breathed" (2 Timothy 3:16), in that it is inspired by God and has its origins in God. It is not just the ideas, but also the words that are inspired by God (1 Corinthians 2:13). All of which leads to a further question.

Why do we need to engage with the Bible. We do so because it is capable of being understood by all God's people. God the Holy Spirit enlightens the minds of Christians Disciples, so that they can understand spiritual truths (1 Corinthians 2:10-16). Through interacting with the Bible, the Church teaches, rebukes, corrects and trains people for the purpose of righteousness (2 Timothy 3:16).

By interacting with the Bible, Christians can be kept from sinning (Psalm 119:11), are comforted (Psalm 119:52), have their minds focused on God (Psalm 43:3) and are sustained in a daily spiritual life (Deuteronomy 8:3). Christians, the Church, also interact with the Bible, because the Bible is a link to the apostles (New Testament) and prophets (Old Testament), who were, and are, the foundation of the Church to which they belong and are an inherent part (Ephesians 2:20).

What is the interaction?

There are five main ways in which Christian Disciples can interact with the Bible. Public reading of Scripture was regular in Israel and in the early Church (Nehemiah 8:3; 2 Peter 3:15).

At the present time, due to high literacy particularly in the Western world and the translation of the scripture into many languages, Scripture can easily be read in private as well as corporately. Memorization of the Bible was commended to "lay up His words in your heart" (Job 22:22).

By reading and memorizing the Bible and meditating on one learns the implications of life's occurrences and God's blessings (Joshua 1:8). These three interactions lead to a fourth: that of obedience. By obeying the Bible, the Christian Disciple learns to obey God, as it is His word (Deuteronomy 31:12).

Fifthly, preaching/teaching of the Bible receives the main emphasis in the New Testament, such as at the Church's birth and Peter's address to the crowd (Acts 2). After they were dispersed due to persecution, the Apostles continued preaching and teaching (Acts 8:4). Luke gives thirteen different words for preaching, and over thirty are used in the entire New Testament. Preaching is defined as God communicating Himself to man through other humans empowered by the Holy Spirit. Preaching of God's Word should be the centrepiece of worship to God in the power of the Holy Spirit.

These four marks of the Church (one, holy, catholic and apostolic) can be summarized like this. The Church is one because Jesus is one; the Church is holy because Jesus is holy; the Church is catholic because Jesus is Saviour of all; the Church is apostolic because, as the Father sent Jesus who taught the Apostles, Jesus sends us to teach the Apostles' teachings. It is these four hallmarks and their functions that are the test of whether a Church is a biblical Church.

1.6. The Church Is Community

[16] "'I am sending you out like sheep among wolves. Therefore, be as shrewd as snakes and as innocent as doves.'" (Matthew 10:16)

How should individual Christian Disciples react regarding a life of Discipleship, in an age where Church attendance is rapidly declining in some parts of the world, particularly the more developed part of the world? It is by being a radical community of radical individuals, which will help stop this decline in Britain and similar places. The Church needs Christian Disciples to be living a "radical Discipleship", engaging with the culture, counting the cost of Discipleship and reflecting true humanity.

Radical Community

Firstly, the Church needs to be a community that is seen to be radical by the surrounding society. At Pentecost, the Church began when the Holy Spirit filled the Disciples (Acts 2:4). This momentous occasion started the Discipleship process of how Christians were learning to live as God's people.

The hallmarks of that community were commitment and transformation. That community was radical. It was where lives of people were being changed as the Holy Spirit filled them. Instead of being a withdrawn people filled with fear of retribution from the Roman government and Jewish leaders, they became a people filled with boldness and joy. The New Testament Church grew by being a radical community full of radical individuals engaging with others. The Church today, is a result of their faithfulness to Jesus Christ.

Today's Church will grow by building a strong community. A community which involves joining together isolated and solitary individuals, where people are full of love, showing care to each other, particularly the frail, elderly and young, with what a creative craving to do what is difficult.

An inherent human need is the need to belong, and by fulfilling relational needs, the radical community will become relevant to the people within it. It will then also become relevant to those who are on the outside and looking in. This involves improving present conditions within society, rather than remaining a conservative community, which merely repairs the status quo. In doing this, today's Church will be emulating characteristics of the early Church (Acts 2:44-45).

As individuals became Christian Disciples, they were added to the Church. Discipline helped ensure that the community was being seen as a holy community. To be excommunicated from the community for gross sin was a severe punishment. However, Church discipline is not primarily about punishment, but rather a "formative and corrective" service as part of Discipleship. Church discipline is foundational to Discipleship making, because it concerns the community's spiritual health, and strengthens the community bonds.

The Church must be a community of Christian Disciples, willing to be holy and seen to be different. It is by being holy, that the Church will grow. The role of the community engaged in radical Christian Discipleship is to help people to be holy and not merely happy. Happiness will flow from holiness, but holiness will not necessarily flow from an induced 'feel good factor'. The radical community needs to be developing Christian Disciples who are trained and equipped so that they can develop Disciples themselves. Whereas in the past, Discipleship processes and programs have emerged after people have joined the Church, they should be foundational. The best way is for the leadership to set the example and show a way forward. Good leadership has good accountability to each other and to the whole community.

Radical Discipleship & Radical Leadership

A radical community requires radical discipleship. Radical discipleship commences with compassion, similar to that of Jesus when he looked over the crowds and commented that they were like sheep without a shepherd (Matthew 9:36).

It should be a compassion driven like that of Jesus towards the woman at the well (John 4:1-26). With compassion as motivation, and a contrite heart, the radical Church community can reach out to the increasing number of those in many developed societies who tend to see Jesus and the Church as irrelevant.

A radical Christian Disciple needs also to involve the voices of others by engaging in dialogue with trusted others. This will involve having a diverse team in the Church who are both willing and empowered to give advice. This team will require an individual leader to have a relaxed grip on control, with power delegated to others, which is radical in that it goes against current styles of leadership.

This radical leadership style requires a pursuit of relationship in order to work, rather than a pursuit of aims and outcomes. This will enable trust to form and helps establish the community on a firm relational foundation. Once relationships have been formed the spiritual gifts of the Christian Disciples can be used to serve the internal and external communities. Exercising gifts and being functional enables the Christian Disciple to grow, be used by God and to flourish with confidence. Radical leadership and radical

Christian Discipleship encourage fringe members.

Finally, Jesus recommends that Christian Disciples be wise like serpent and innocent as doves (Matthew 10:16). That means Christian Disciples are to be skilful and shrewd in making decisions that are characterized by intelligence, patience and shrewdness. Is that your experience or observation?

Additionally, Christian Disciples are to be gentle and harmless, like doves. This would develop Christian Disciples and leaders who would be accountable to others to live a life of integrity worthy of the gospel (Philippians 1:27).

This is a life, which is seen to be as holy and blameless. In order to do this, dependence on the Holy Spirit for strength and care is a necessity. By relying on the Holy Spirit, the Christian Disciple is perpetually connected to Jesus Christ, who is the Head of the Church community.

The Christian Disciple in a position of authority is to be a shepherd leader rather than a manager. Why? So, guidance and nurture are central, rather than only feeding the community.

A Christian Disciple who cares and loves is one who goes out to find the lost rather than waiting for the lost to come. This shepherd is also involved in the training of other Christian Disciples so that care is disseminated.

This does not mean however that a radical Christian Disciple leader becomes a subordinate to the community, catering to every whim and fad suggested by others. The Christian Disciple leader needs be a servant but also requires discernment.

Discipleship at most Churches these days is organized around their programmes of small groups, Sunday services, prayer groups, leadership group and opportunities to serve. Discipleship in these Churches usually involves some form of leadership accountability in four key areas:

Mission, Maturity, Outreach and Leadership. Mission involves helping people become Christian and nurturing their faith diligently.

If Western Churches and Christian Disciples started to take radical steps, both in being and making Christian Disciples, then growth would systematically follow. The Church would no longer be seen as irrelevant but as a thriving community. A community of believers where Jesus is glorified, and transformation is sought and encouraged.

Stand Alone

[18] "If the world hates you, keep in mind that it hated me first. [19] If you belonged to the world, it would love you as its own. As it is, you do not belong to the world, but I have chosen you out of the world. That is why the world hates you. [20] Remember what I told you: "A servant is not greater than His master." If they persecuted me, they will persecute you also. If they obeyed my teaching, they will obey yours also. [21] They will treat you this way because of my name, for they do not know the one who sent me."
(John 15:18-21)

We have a new identity as Christians. What are we to do with it? We are to remain faithful to Jesus, despite difficult times. It means staying faithful to Him, regardless of opposition and alternatives. By doing this we are standing alone and being faithful to Him. Being faithful to the God we proclaim as our King and our Saviour. Satan brings pressure to bear on Christians to reduce their standards and commitment.

Christian Disciples undergo challenges from the world that doesn't like or understand us and constantly tempts us to do wrong things or not to do right things. We are to be separate from sin but not separated from a sinful society. This is what Jesus meant when He said we are to be "in the world but not of the world" (John 17:11, 15-19).

The key to standing alone is through constant identification with Jesus Christ in lifestyle and words. However, as we live out our Christian life, as Christian Disciples we will face hindrances to identifying with Jesus. Here are just three major areas that as Christian Disciples, we all have to struggle through. There is an inborn fear of what others will think - fear of being different and being laughed at. Then there is the fear of losing family and friends. To have the right friends however, a person must be willing to have enemies. Jesus made friends on the basis of who would accept Him and His message. We may be excluded from the company of those who reject Jesus (Luke 6:26). Then finally, there is the desire to be like those in the world. An example of this is provided by David in Psalm 73, where he envied the success of the godless. This was until he realized their destiny was disaster; and that he had God and needed nothing else. Always taking what is best is no sacrifice.

If they are some of the hindrances, what are some of the keys in battling these hindrances? As Christian Disciples we have to remember God's way of life is superior. It is a life filled with abundance according to Jesus in John 10:10. Then we realise that acting as light and salt in the world, we are co-operating with God and He is being glorified according to Peter in 1 Peter 4:12-14). Remember; if you give people no reason to ask about the hope and faith you have in Jesus, they probably won't ask. Jesus warned His Disciples in the upper room the night before His death that the world would hate them and persecute them (John 15:18-20).

How then can we verbally identify with Jesus? Never apologize for what you know and believe to be a superior way of life. However, that does not mean to be smug and arrogant about it because we are commanded to walk humbly and meekly. Just be natural about it. As a college principle told me a long time ago - and I still remember the words - "Let your spiritual life be natural and your natural life be spiritual." One way to do this is to hold tight to the idea that you are not your own boss - Jesus is your Lord and let him take both the strain and glory. Remember that those who reject you also reject Jesus.

Another area of the Christian life is in making right decisions in questionable areas. Imagine you are in a difficult situation and you have to make a correct decision in a questionable area. What do you do? Why not you ask yourself the following questions and make statements to yourself. Does it bring glory to God (1 Corinthians 10:31)? Can I thank God for this activity? Could Jesus accompany me in it? Does it build my Christian character (1 Corinthians 10:23-24)? Will it cause another Christian to sin and therefore stumble (1 Corinthians 8:9-13)? This activity or inactivity, should not control habitually (1 Corinthians 6:12) and if in doubt, throw it out (Romans 14:22-23). We can ask other people, particularly other Christians, for advice. It is important what other people think, for we are to abstain from all appearances of evil (1 Thessalonians 5:22). Overall, we are to rely on the Holy Spirit to help and ask for His help and guidance.

2.1. What Is The Internet & What Does It Look Like?

Since the advent of the Internet in 1957 and the subsequent arrival of the home Personal Computer and the World Wide Web (WWW), people have been using these tools for a myriad of reasons including research, education and communication.

With this increase of communication, it was not long until Internet communities were formed. These communities could be broken down into three kinds:

- subjective (people gathering with similar interests);

- objective (a gathering of people affected by similar interests);

- defining authority (people gathering whose identity was formed by allegiance to a common authority).

However, some critics dismiss the concept due to it being by definition, text and image based and full of self-interest. Others argue that they can become closed and subjective. However, that is true of any kind of community – virtual or not. Juxtaposed to these concepts is the knowledge that technology is advancing with greater methods of interaction becoming available and global barriers collapsing which make communication and understanding between global citizens possible. With these virtual communities came the world of 'Digital Space', to coexist with physical reality.

It is suggested by some people that the Internet or Digital Space, is a computer-simulated environment with which people are able to interact almost as if it were part of the physical world. This Internet, or Digital Space as it is also known, is a model of social interaction. This the Internet is where time, space and body are transcended in which to form relationships. However, these relationships are not limited to being within Digital Space but have some links to the world offline – the physical reality as it were. Digital Space and offline interest cannot be precisely divorced from each other due to the import of offline interest to a Digital Space. In doing this, people of similar interests, or enquiring after spiritual matters, are able to bring offline interests to the world of Digital Space. It is here that an Internet Church can thrive, educate, inform and satisfy.

As the Church continues through the twenty-first century, and as technology marches inexorably onwards, a new kind of Church has been birthed. This is a Church that does not meet in a specific physical locale but gathers in an Internet environment.

Can God interact in a 'Digital Space Environment'?

Naturally a question now arises. "Is it possible for God to interact with people in a 'Digital Space Environment'? I have heard respected Bible teachers say that virtual worship equates with a virtual God. They say things like "Worship in a 'Digital Space Environment' is not worship to the Almighty God of Scripture."

Some people questions the idea that the Internet can be considered a sacred space due to its inability to "communicate blessedness like that of a cathedral. However, we know from Scripture that it is the presence of Christ in people's hearts that makes the Church, and not a building with four walls. Jesus promised that where His followers meet in His name, He would be there (Matthew

18:20). The Church therefore is not a building but a continuance of Jesus' anointing by the Holy Spirit.

God operates within the hearts of people by His Spirit (Galatians 4:6) and is not confined to the four walls of a 'sacred' building (Acts 17:24). It is in people's hearts that His light shines the knowledge of His glory (2 Corinthians 4:6). But what is community? For the Church Father, Augustine, community is a harmonious collection of individuals. This most certainly describes an online community where a group of Christians are meeting in Digital Space. They are meeting especially in order to discuss Scripture, worship Almighty God and pray to their God and Saviour in the majestic name of Jesus Christ in the power of the indwelling Holy Spirit.

People interact with other people all the time within a 'Digital Space Environment'. If people can do that, then certainly the God who is outside of time and space is able to interact with them. Indeed, God can and does interact within a 'Digital Space Environment', because He works within the hearts, minds and will of people, and is not restricted by physical barriers.

Many people have come to a living faith in Jesus Christ in all forms of 'Digital Space Environments'. Using a computer, listening to a radio, watching television, reading a book or a letter or indeed reading Scripture itself, are also forms of 'Digital Space'. For example, reading a book - unless you have the author present in the room, are you not engaging with the author in a "virtual" environment and reading His written thoughts? God has used written literature down through the ages, in order to interact with people. This would of course include the Bible, His written Word.

Just as people, even arch-critics of Church in 'Digital Space Environment's would admit, that when listening to a CD of religious songs in the privacy of their own home is worship and that God interacts with them. Yet, is not that musical CD a basic form of 'Digital Space Environment'? Therefore, it must be said that God has and still does interact within a 'Digital Space Environment' – even with those who deny that He does. But does that mean that Church located in a 'Digital Space Environment' is still Church and moreover, part of the historical Church? To help us understand this concept further, here it is illustrated.

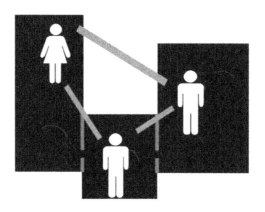

Physical Church

How people see Physical Church: as people who are connected.

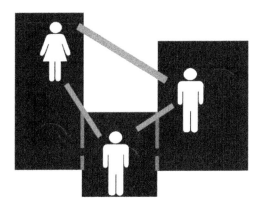

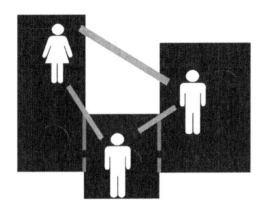

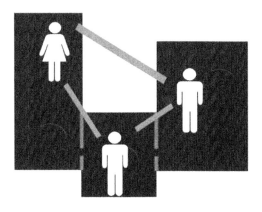

What is an Internet Church?

A good place to start is to ask the question, "What is an Internet Church?" Let's start with some words from Hebrews.

"And let us consider one another in order to stir up love and good works, not forsaking the assembling of ourselves together, as is the manner of some, but exhorting one another, and so much the more as you see the Day approaching." (Hebrews 10:24-25)

Therefore, another question. How can those people who are housebound or geographically isolated, assemble with others as the writer to Hebrews commands? This is particularly pertinent if the geographically centred local Churches do not have the resources to collect these people for worship services and other meetings. What can be done to ensure that these groups of people are not isolated further from an active, and indeed interactive, Church life?

Computer based communities are 'Internet Environments', whereby the community members interact with each other. The best way is through an 'Internet Environment', as established in an online Church, where Jesus Christ is glorified, preached and worshipped. This is an Internet Church. If a person can get to a normal geographically based local Church, then I would always urge that person to go to that Church, as well as an Internet Church.

However, if for some reason you are unable to attend a geographically located Church, then an Internet Church is where you can have fellowship with other Christians. In doing so you will be encouraged, growing in grace and maturity together and rejoicing together in the fellowship of believers. You would be part of a fellowship of believers, meeting in an Internet environment for a variety of reasons.

This Internet Church would have a common purpose (Psalm 133:1-3), a common belief (Acts 2:42), a common hope (Hebrews 11:39-40) and finally, a sharing of needs (2 Corinthians 8:1-15). Just as all Christians have fellowship with the Father (1 John 1:3), Jesus (1 Corinthians 1:9) and the Holy Spirit (Philippians 2:1), so they also have fellowship with each other (1 John 1:7). This fellowship is with each other, regardless of their individual geographical location, in a 'Digital Space Environment'. An Internet Church is an Internet website, where people, quite possibly geographically dispersed, gather together for fellowship, teaching, mission & worship, like the way people have congregated since Pentecost. This is distinct from a Church website which contains information about itself, the Gospel and/or its own denominational dogma.

Currently, at least to my knowledge, there are three main types of Internet Church, all with some form of audio-visual capability and community interaction. Firstly, those that are primarily text based. Secondly, there are Churches with a two-dimensional graphical interface, text and some sound for use in worship and prayers. Thirdly, Churches with a fully three-dimensional graphical viewing interface, with full sound and interactivity. While these three examples usually require registration in order to show commitment to the ethos and core values, guest passes are available. These guest passes allow countless others to watch the Internet Church service and participate in discussion afterwards.

Now another question naturally arises. How can an Internet Church operate regarding to fellowship, mission, bible teaching and worship? For it is by doing those four things, that any Church, whether located geographically or within a 'Digital Space Environment', can lay claim to being part of the historical one, holy, catholic and apostolic Church.

Function of an Internet Church

How can an Internet Church function regarding fellowship, mission, bible teaching and worship? The phrase *'one holy, catholic and apostolic'* probably remains the best means of identifying whether a Church is truly part of the historical Church or not. The Church at its inception was a practice of shared faith, epitomized by these dynamic marks. Although definitions may vary, these hallmarks traverse the broad spectrum of Christendom in the Orthodox, Roman Catholic and Protestant traditions. The term 'one holy, catholic and apostolic Church' is a verbal confession, denoting the four visible dimensions of the invisible Church and being a community springing forth from its first century founding. Furthermore, it evolves from generation to generation, but without losing the core beliefs. Catholic in this context means 'universal' and not the denomination or tradition.

> [17] Sanctify them by the truth; your word is truth. [18] As you sent me into the world, I have sent them into the world. [19] For them I sanctify myself, that they too may be truly sanctified.
> [20] "My prayer is not for them alone. I pray also for those who will believe in me through their message, [21] that all of them may be one, Father, just as you are in me and I am in you. May they also be in us so that the world may believe that you have sent me. (John 17:17-21)

In these Scriptures showing Jesus at prayer, we see that Jesus stipulates these four hallmarks of His Church: one (John 17:21); holy (John 17:17, 19); catholic (John 17:21); apostolic (John 17:18). By engaging in fellowship, worship, mission and bible teaching, a Church thereby reflects the historical and biblical universal Church, which is one, holy, catholic and apostolic. One in that the Church exhibits fellowship between the individual believer and God the Father, God the Son and God the Holy Spirit; as well as fellowship between believers. A Church is holy in that the Church encourages worship of Almighty God. Catholic in that, the Church is engaged in the continuous mission of evangelisation. Finally, the Church is apostolic in that it teaches from the Bible.

While these four hallmarks are statements of faith, they also must lead to declarations of function, because the Church must be actively visible. These four derived functions of the Church are: fellowship, worship, mission and bible interaction. They are mutually interdependent and are a visible exhibition of the invisible Church.

How does an Internet Church engage in Fellowship? Fellowship is a mutual sharing together, which is seen in the sharing of stories and interacting with other Christians. This is also one way an Internet Church, engages in acts of fellowship, just as all Churches do. Sharing a common purpose of seeking Jesus, worshipping and praying together, playing games, engaging in stimulating dialogues and lending support when required, are all facets of Internet Church fellowship. The Internet Church can also engage in regular offline meetings to help engage each other people more.

How does an Internet Church engage in worship? Worship in an Internet Church has a variety of methods in which God's glorification is sought. Global worship includes singing, responsive prayers and liturgy. Each individual member having His or her own bread and wine can engage in the Eucharist, similar to traditional Church. A problem may well arise with baptism which is, by necessity, a physical action. This problem can be overcome by negotiating with a traditional Church to baptise the person wanting baptism.

How does an Internet Church engage in mission? Internet Church evangelism is primarily based on a friendship evangelism model with building relationships at its core. It is talking to people online, interacting through blogs, writing of testimonies, engaging in discussion threads and venturing into other online fora and communities. In an Internet Church, where people are judged more on the ability to be persuasive rather than appearance, Scripture is powerful. Evangelism is therefore not instantaneous (although it can be) but rather a process of journey.

How does an Internet Church engage in teaching? In an Internet Church bible teaching continues to be central. Sermons are preached, and interactive discussions are engaged in afterwards. Topical teaching and blog threads can teach Scripture, be commented upon and subsequently discussed. Video and audio files can be streamed or downloaded from the Church and played on portable devices, for use in personal time. Particularly relevant is the narrative style when online "holographic stimulation" will facilitate emotional attachment. So, if that is how an Internet Church functions, what are some of the liabilities of an Internet Church?

2.2. Liabilities of Internet Church

Having seen briefly how an Internet Church may function, we go on assess our next question. What are the liabilities of an Internet Church? There are perhaps three main perceived weaknesses of an Internet Church as expressed by its critics. Let's look briefly at them and consider ways in which an Internet Church can help overcome them. These three main liabilities are Anonymity, the idea that Virtual Communities are not genuine communities, and .Internet Addiction.

Anonymity is a bad thing

Anonymity of the person on the internet provides the opportunity to escape from emotional difficulties such as depression, stress, anxiety, or a relationship or family problem. Anonymity can be used for deceitful practices and to prey on the weak and vulnerable. Whilst these can be true, at least in part, anonymity is not necessarily a bad thing. Anonymity, within an Internet Environment, including Internet Churches, can help people overcome shyness, social awkwardness and instil confidence and be encouraging.

While anonymity certainly can help people to be dishonest and deceitful, it can also be a safe place where people feel that they can be more honest about themselves. This leads these people to be being more open and honest when engaging with others in Digital Space. As that person interacts and has fellowship with others in an Internet community, this may well help give them confidence to deal with people in a physical reality which may be lacking.

Anonymity also did not prevent people seeking help, advice and sharing problems. Particularly young people still developing and growing as people. These young people being able to ask awkward questions about life anonymously can be of considerable help and assistance. Placing anonymous prayer requests in an Internet community, particularly for illnesses, troubles and circumstances which are embarrassing, is of course a massive leap forward for some people who otherwise may not ask anybody else to pray their petitions.

Virtual Community is not real community

Now let us face what is for some at least is the biggest liability – the idea that the Internet is not real community or fellowship. Some critics of the Internet Communities insist that all online interaction is purely about the transmission of information.

However, when information is being transferred or communicated, this usually has some form of psychological effect and can affect emotions and psyche in both a negative and positive sense. Therefore, to say that it is solely about information transference is endemically wrong.

Critics may also categorically deny the legitimacy of the Internet Environment communities because there is a distinct lack of obligation and accountability between people. Within an Internet Church Community, there will be terms and conditions for a person to read and agree with prior to registration. Therefore, the person will be entering into a covenant with fellow users and is therefore accountable to them. Any misdemeanours in Internet Church communities, should be looked at and dealt with swiftly.

Real community used to be seen as geographically centred. However, with the advent of the Internet Environment community, this is no longer the case. Etymologically, community has returned to its original concept based on social grouping and quality of relationship. All Internet Churches probably will have a wide geographical spread due to its very nature: being on the World Wide Web or Internet. This does not preclude, however, that giving and receiving help and assistance ceases. So virtual community is far more than information transference, as some may insist, but rather it consists of, amongst other things, mutual giving and receiving of care and assistance.

Internet Addiction

Firstly, for some people there may well be a level of Internet addiction. This could become a problem within an Internet Church environment. One reason for Internet addiction is escapism from real life problems. Other signs of internet addiction could be the person growing moody and irritable when they are unable to go online. It could also be that they are addicted to an alter-ego in an Internet Environment that acts and behaves different from offline life.

When discovered, the person would need to be encouraged to seek some form of counselling or be given pastoral care. A cure is possible but a need to recognize the problem is the obvious first step. Other steps to overcome this addiction would include waiting for the plea to help, rationing time spent on Digital Space, supervision when engaging in on the Internet and in severe cases, suspension and prohibition from engaging in a Digital Space. Internet Church operators may need to monitor people's time spent online. The addicted individual may need to consider the spiritual discipline of fasting from Internet access in order to regain power over their addiction. If they are unable to do this, then traditional Church may well be a better model for them to attend, if at all possible.

2.3. Benefits of Internet Church

If those are the three main liabilities of engaging in a Digital Space, our next question to answer is what are some of the benefits? Internet Church can provide a spiritual avenue for people not currently able to attend a traditional geographical Church in order to participate in the function of mission, worship, fellowship and bible teaching. It is a major benefit can be seen in giving to the isolated and detached of society with an imaginative desire to achieve the impossible. That is a task for an Internet Church community to grasp and proceed with.

Assisting Housebound & disabled people

One of the ways in which an Internet Church is effective is in the area of helping housebound and disabled people. Housebound people, including those with physical, emotional and psychological problems, may only venture from their domicile on rare occasions. Access to a traditional geographical based Church is not always catered for, as well as people being too shy to attend traditional Church. Indeed, I know a lady, who because she has a low self-esteem, she felt more at ease communicating in an Internet environment, particularly in an Internet Church. I dare say she is not alone in feeling and thinking like that. I am sure you know people how are just like her.

If the local geographically based Churches do not have transport for housebound and disabled people, then an Internet Church could well be the means to allow these people to participate in the life of the Church. By using technology, housebound and disabled people would be able to participate a great deal within an Internet Church environment, including fellowship and worship. There is also the possibility of extending their participation to serving the Internet Church in some capacity such as moderator, administrator or helping to lead worship, bible teaching and prayer times.

This inevitably leads to confidence dealing with people offline in a physical reality. Additionally, it also can lead to exhibiting faith in God, by desiring to serve Him and the Church by using their Spiritual gifts. Spiritual gifts which until then may well be lying dormant and unused. In doing this people will develop confidence in themselves. Instead of feeling neglected, isolated and alone, they may feel wanted, and more importantly, loved by others. One major foreseeable problem with this proposal is that it may be prohibitively expensive to arrange and operate these schemes. There is also the requirement of sourcing technical support in the case of hardware and software malfunction. Training issues could be another issue.

However, with God, if He is in the planning, nothing is impossible. Local Church groups, Christian organizations and denominations could pool financial and personnel resources, so they could be achieved. It would signify visually that Churches have unity, even without uniformity. It would also give rise to the opportunity for traditional Churches to work along with Internet Churches to the glory of God. Charities and Government help is also widely available to help subside costs or donate technology. In helping the housebound, the Internet Church will have extended the Gospel's reach and be seen to be obedient to that ancient command to "love your neighbour as yourself." (Matthew 22:39).

Assisting the Geographically Isolated

An Internet Church would enable isolated Church communities, such as those ministered to by Bush Church

Aid Society of Australia[3]. This method would enable such organizations to fulfil their vision.

Bush Church Aid Society of Australia

Similar links could be created with isolated Christian communities and Churches in Great Britain or the USA. This would be similar to the way New Testament Churches linked. The New Testament communities linked for the following reasons: prayer support, encouragement, imitation and theological reflection. Today, isolated Churches can also gather together for fellowship, worship, evangelism and teaching in an Internet Church.

Another benefit is for Christians in persecuted countries to meet with Christians world-wide. This of course may give additional problems given the Internet censorship policy of some countries. An Internet Church can enable Christians to communicate and worship together from a vast geographical area, where there may not be many Churches or other Christians – if any at all. This is self-evident given the scope and range of the Internet. Consequently, the enabling of housebound, disabled and

---

[3] http://www.bushChurchaid.com.au

geographically isolated people to engage with other Christians is a major benefit of an Internet Church. Without Internet Church a lot of people and their spiritual gifting would go missing from life within the one, holy catholic and apostolic Church.

2.4. What Can An Internet Church Service Look Like?

A Church service on the Internet can take many shapes and forms, as well as varying lengths of time. People can come in and out when they like, without causing disruption.

On the following pages, for the sake of brevity, is just one example of how an Internet Church can gather. This is an Internet Church service between 2 people. They can of course, be used with more people attending. Rabi was in India and I was in the UK.

Other ways to gather as Internet Church include via live video link or pre-recorded video gathered in one place such as Facebook or YouTube.

Greetings

23/10/2016 15:15 - Rabi
Welcome to WOWChurch Facebook! I am Rabi from India. Before we begin, please do ensure the sound on your device is
working! There will be YouTube[4] clips.

23/10/2016 15:15 - Davo
G'day! Dave from Australia here!

---

[4] YouTube is a popular video sharing website on the internet where videos can be viewed. http://www.youtube.com

Opening Prayer

23/10/2016 15:16 - Rabi
Let's start with a brief silence to prepare our minds and hearts before God. Then I will say a short prayer, to which you read in an attitude of prayer and respond Amen afterwards. When you have put Amen, we will move on with the service. Thanks...

23/10/2016 15:20 - Rabi
Father, as we commence, let our hearts and minds be right before you. We thank for your Son Jesus. It's in His name we offer you these praises, prayers and petitions in the power of the Holy Spirit who lives inside those who are your children. Amen

23/10/2016 15:21 - Davo
Amen

Praise Time

23/10/2016 15:21 - Rabi
Now, let's say this prayer together. After you have prayed it yourself, please do say a short sentence of praise to God

23/10/2016 15:21 - Rabi

Our God, God of all people! God of heaven and earth, seas and rivers, God of sun and moon, of all the stars, God of high mountain and lowly valley, God over heaven, and in heaven, and under heaven. He has a dwelling in heaven and earth and sea and in all things that are in them. He inspires all things; He quickens all things. He is over all things; he supports all things.

He makes the light of the sun to shine, He surrounds the moon and the stars, He has made wells in the arid earth, Placed dry islands in the sea. He has a Son co-eternal with himself... And the Holy Spirit breathes in them; Not separate are the Father and the Son and the Holy Spirit.

23/10/2016 15:23 - Davo
Amen. Father we praise you for your abundance in all things.

 23/10/2016 15:22 - Rabi
O Great God! Thank you, that You are love and that you love me and have adopted me into Your family...
Thank for WOWing me regularly...

Song

23/10/2016 15:23 - Rabi

Here is a song! After you have watched the video (or sung it!), please do offer up some words of praise to God.

If for some reason words are failing you, simple say "Lord God, I lift up thanks and praise to you alone."

Then after a short time, I will wrap up this section with a short prayer.

https://www.youtube.com/watch?v=rcRtZyfTxX4

23/10/2016 15:26 - Rabi
Praise be to you O God that you desire me to know you and be a witness for you in this world... WOW!
"Father God, accept these praises as sweet smelling perfume! Amen!"

23/10/2016 15:28 - Davo
Lord, praise you for allowing me to come into your presence. Into Your Holiness. Praise you for Your Son who has made me righteous in your eyes! Amen

23/10/2016 15:28 - Rabi
Amen

Bible Readings

23/10/2016 15:29 - Rabi
We now have our Bible readings...
When you have finished reading each
of them, please do put a one word
response of your choice.
Zechariah 8:15-17 - Now I am
determined to bless Jerusalem and the
people of Judah. So don't be afraid.
This is what you must do: Tell the truth
to each other. Render verdicts in your
courts that are just and that lead to
peace. Don't scheme against each
other. Stop your love of telling lies that
you swear are the truth. I hate all these
things, says the LORD."

23/10/2016 15:29 - Davo
Truth
Honesty

23/10/2016 15:29 - Rabi
Justice!

23/10/2016 15:30 - Rabi
Matthew 22:36-40 - "Teacher, which is the most important commandment in the law of Moses?"
Jesus replied, "'You must love the LORD your God with all your heart, all your soul, and all your mind.' This is the first and greatest commandment. A second is equally important: 'Love your neighbour as yourself.' The entire law and all the demands of the prophets are based on these two commandments."

23/10/2016 15:30 - Davo
Obey

23/10/2016 15:30 - Rabi
Fruit...

Teaching

23/10/2016 15:30 - Rabi

Now we will have our teaching. Today we have another WOW Word! When you have finished watching, please do write a short sentence about something that struck you from this teaching

https://www.youtube.com/watch?v=I8e
TdTxxVNO

23/10/2016 15:40 - Rabi
Lord, help me to love all others I meet as you love me...

23/10/2016 15:41 - Davo
Father help me to love even those I don't like!

Prayer Time

23/10/2016 15:41 - Rabi
We say a series of prayers now. Please do reply Amen when you have prayed. O Great God our provider, for those who are ill, we ask for a healing touch and wisdom for the medical staff treating them. Father, be the strength for all those who are grieving and mourning the loss of loved ones. We pray that those in despair will be helped and where there is darkness there will be light. O Lord God, give strength to the weak.

23/10/2016 15:42 - Davo
Amen

23/10/2016 15:42 - Rabi
Amen O God

23/10/2016 15:43 - Rabi
Father, we lift before you, all those facing challenging situations: such as loneliness, confinement at home, geographical isolation, lack of employment, health issues, and financial pressures.
O Father, please meet their needs in whatever challenging situation is being faced, and we put ourselves in your hands to help meet those needs where we can.

23/10/2016 15:43 - Davo
Let us be your hands and feet, O Lord. Amen

23/10/2016 15:43 - Rabi
Amen O God

23/10/2016 15:43 - Rabi
We ask these things, our Father God, in the name of your Son, Jesus Christ, and in the power of the Holy Spirit. Amen!

23/10/2016 15:44 - Davo
Amen and amen!

Closing Prayer

23/10/2016 15:44 - Rabi
Let's close now with this short prayer, and please say Amen when you have prayed. Thanks!
Jesus the Lord is risen from the dead! He is risen indeed! All praise be to God the Father, God the Son and God the Holy Spirit.
Continue to be with us, o great God and help us and those we love.
Amen

23/10/2016 15:44 - Davo
Amen

23/10/2016 15:44 - Rabi Choudhoury
May it be so, O great God - Father, Son
and Spirit!

23/10/2016 15:45 - Davo
Amen

23/10/2016 15:45 Rabi Choudhoury
Dave! Thanks for joining me on
WOWChurch today! Have a blessed and
great day, my brother.

23/10/2016 15:45 - Davo
Thank you, Rabi! Praise God for you.

Section 3: Development

3.1. Use Your Creativity

Our God is a creative God! His creativity is all around us! Further to this, as humans we are created in His image, and thus, we are creative! Everybody has some form of significant creative potential. If you don't think you do, perhaps it is because you haven't found your creative niche yet! You only need to look at a child playing, and you will soon see their innate creativity at work. The natural creativity of children is amazing!

We are to develop this creativity within us, and also to help others to develop their own creativity. However, quite frequently significant persons bury creativity under layers of conditioning and negativity. Some of the greatest culprits are teachers, parents and peers, but there is hope because the conditioning process can be reversed. It is a process with a high cost factor, because creativity is essentially a lifestyle. It has to pervade every area of your experience. None more so than in your area of service as a Christian Disciple!

Examples of Biblical creativity

Jesus used creativity in His teaching! He took everyday people and objects, creating lessons out of them. Think of some of your favourite parables and see the creativity behind them! As for the Psalms, they are filled with creative language in order to praise God, seeking penance before God and expressing a desire to know God better!

Similarly, some of the symbolic language of the Bible is very creative. Take for example the genealogy of Matthew 1. To us it may well be tedious and insignificant, but to its initial audience of a small group of Jewish believers, it includes enormous significance and creative symbolism! The way Matthew constructed the genealogy highlights many things, one of which was His highlighting of Abraham, David and of course, Jesus! We know that to the Jewish mind at that time, numbers were not just mathematically significant but also held great symbolism! For example, the number seven was thought to represent perfection. Each of the 3 stages in the genealogy of Matthew 1 contains 14 stages making a total of 42 times perfection! So what Matthew was saying, at least symbolically, that Jesus was a great deal more than perfect! Now if you were not a first century Jew, you would not at first see this creative symbolism!

Why the importance of creativity?

Creativity perpetuates the learning process. As long as you live, you should be learning and remember that Christian Discipleship is essentially a call to perpetual learning. Not only for discipleship for yourself, but to help others in their own discipleship. I have often told people that there is no such thing as retiring from the Christian life or from the use of their Spiritual Gifts, including their creativity. Creativity is essential to meet the growing demands of a constantly changing society.

Package thinkers are out of business for an impact tomorrow. If we do not prepare those that we lead to change, they will not be a change element in our next generation. The way we do a lot of things today, are not the same as they would have been in 1918 and nor will they be in the year 2118.

Creativity is important to both affect & infect your communication with a characteristic freshness & vitality. We are commanded to communicate the truth. A communicative individual is always a creative individual. Creativity develops your leadership style and it will overhaul your lifestyle. Most Christian Disciples seem to only exist and not live! If a person is living in the past or in the future, they cannot be enjoying the present.

Creativity, as I am sure you are aware, is largely a matter of effort. The mind is like a muscle and grows with use. Quantity is essential to quality in the creative process. Scientific evidence suggests that it is only a maximum of 6% of ideas that are good. You have to get more ideas to get some winning ideas. Results of ideas which are good, bad or indifferent are welcome. Don't pass judgment at the outset of the creativity process; you have to withhold it. Incubation generates illumination. Put your ideas on the back burner. Put time between thinking of ideas. Then don't be surprised when a moment of inspiration of how to complete it arrives! Group effort stimulates creativity if you learn how to listen.

Creativity can be used in the Church. Just take for example worship services. Is worship just singing songs? Or can other means be used in order to worship, such as responsive prayers and bible readings? What about dancing as part of creative worship? What about creative outreach or evangelism? Try something new! By being creative, the Church can be culturally relevant whilst remaining biblically faithful to God.

How to activate creativity?

Experience provides the fuel for ideation, which is the creation and formation of ideas.

- **Involvement in hobbies & fine arts:** For example, photographic sites are great places to see creativity in process and get tips on how to improve! There are oodles of websites out there for almost every conceivable hobby. Social media, such as Facebook or Instagram, are great places to set up a group, be involved in a group and get ideas, critique and to grow in your creativity and gifting. As well as help others to do so.

- **Problem solving:** Get started by getting your drive going in the right direction.
- **Reading:** Creativity thrives on reading. The only problem is passivity. Read it until you can tell somebody else. We tend to read the stuff with which we agree which only serves to reinforce our own prejudices and presuppositions. Read things that you know that you won't necessarily agree with. Expand your reading and thinking. By doing these things, your innate creativity will be stimulated and energised.
- **Spend time with creative people:** Think with those you are leading. You think your ideas are so good because you have never tested them against someone diametrically opposed to yours.
- **Writing:** Keep a journal, a blog or a website! It's easier than you may well think. Write down questions, examples and your meditations.

3.2. Use Your Spiritual Gifts

When Jesus said to His apostles "I tell you the truth, anyone who has faith in me will do what I have been doing. He will do even greater things than these, because I am going to the Father." (John 14:12), it was through the promised Holy Spirit (John 14:17), and the impartation of Spiritual Gifts, that His words were to be fulfilled.

Our first question is to ask what are spiritual gifts? Spiritual Gifts derive from the Greek word *'charismata'*. They are also called grace gifts, which refers to any gift God gives out of the abundance of His grace. They are given to all Christians as God sees fit (1 Corinthians 12:11).

There are four main passages in the New Testament regarding Spiritual Gifts (Romans 12:3-8; 1 Corinthians 12:1-11, 28-31; Ephesians 4:11-13; 1 Peter 4:10-11). The lists of gifts, given in the New Testament are representative of spiritual gifts and are not to be taken as a definitive listing. The gifts quoted in various passages of the New Testament are: "administration, apostleship, discernment, evangelism, exhortation, giving, faith, healing, helps, knowledge, leadership, mercy, miracles, pastor, prophecy, service, teaching, tongues, the interpretation of tongues, wisdom."

To which we may add present day gifts like leading a congregation on keyboard or guitar. As Christian Disciples however, Paul commands that we "try to excel in gifts that build up the Church." (1 Corinthians 14:12). When the Church is built up, unity will inevitably prevail. The diversity of Spiritual gifts within each local Church, helps build unity.

A further question now, is to ask who has Spiritual Gifts? Is it just a select few, judiciously picked out by the Church hierarchy? By no means! All Christian Disciples have Spiritual Gifts, for "in His grace, God has given us different gifts for doing certain things well." (Romans 12:6; 1 Corinthians 12:12-25, 1 Corinthians 14:26). God the Holy Spirit, through His infinite wisdom, mercy and grace bestows these gifts that belong to Him, upon His servants, Christian Disciples, and these gifts are to be used primarily to bring glory to Him! (1 Peter 4:11). They are opportunities for Christian Disciples to serve other people. The person in your church or community, who is housebound has gifts that can be used and developed by the Spirit. Some gifts like teaching, helping or leadership quite possibly are enhancements of natural abilities whilst others like faith, healing and miracles are from the Spirit's empowerment alone.

The purpose and reason that the Holy Spirit imparts spiritual gifts to Christian Disciples is so that the whole body of Christ is built up (Ephesians 4:12), for the common good of the Church (1 Corinthians 12:7, 1 Corinthians 14:12) and finally, "so that in all things God may be praised through Jesus Christ." (1 Peter 4:12)

These three reasons signify that God wants Christian Disciples to be active in service for His glory and the extension of His Kingdom and not to be still like stagnant water. That is why Christian Disciples have been given gifts and abilities. If these gifts are not used for God's purposes, then they are ultimately meaningless and useless. Therefore, what is an appropriate response by Christian Disciples in relation to these gifts?

Discovering Spiritual Gifts

How does a Christian Disciple discover their Spiritual Gifts? As the Bible is primary to spiritual growth and understanding, the Christian Disciple needs to study God's word diligently, enhancing the relationship and building bonds with the Lord. Then the Christian Disciple needs to pray and seek the face of the Lord in deep prayer and meditation. Thirdly by asking the advice and wisdom of the leaders in the Church we attend or from friends who know you well as to where our gifting lies. Lastly, it is also through asking questions of yourself. What do I enjoy? What am I good at? If God blesses what you are doing, and it is fruitful, you may have discovered an area where your spiritual gifting lies!

Christian Disciple's Response

As Christian Disciples, we are dependent upon each other, just as one part of the human body has dependence on another part. That is why we serve each other and use the gifts generously given by God. As all Christian Disciples have gifts, we have a responsibility to discover and develop them (1 Timothy 4:14)! God has called out for himself Christian Disciples and equipped them with spiritual gifts, and they are not to be neglected! We are to discover, discern, develop and put into effect our spiritual gifts, so that God can be glorified, and His Church built up!

As we are not to neglect our gifts, or let other Christian Disciples neglect their gifts, we are to fan the gift into flame (2 Timothy 1:6), much like blowing on embers and stirring them up will restart the flames of a fire! To do this Christian Disciples are to employ their gift faithfully by asking God to continue their development, strengthening and opportunities to use them! Christians are to seek gifts that build up others, commands Paul (1 Corinthians 14:1-12). Ask God faithfully for gifts that give opportunity for service to God and others!

3.3. Be At Prayer

Prayer, as I am sure you know, along with the Bible, are our weapons in spiritual warfare! Why? I wonder when you last said "Good morning" to God as you woke up or said "Good night" to God as you fell asleep. Prayer is at the centre in the relationship between God and the Christian Disciple. It is the major action of fellowship between God and humans, and of humans communicating with God, both in talking and listening (Genesis 18:33).

Prayer is also a way of "letting God in" to the life of the Christian Disciple, and of enjoying the company of God, relating all aspects of life to Him. Prayer is also a means of protection for the Christian Disciple, in that the Christian Disciple is too weak in their own understanding and strength to withstand all that is against them. God Himself assists the Christian Disciple as they pray: where yearnings are corrected and strengthened. Prayers expressing desires and thoughts offer a contributory way to the journey of the Christian Disciple.

The Lord's Prayer and the book of Psalms are superb biblical examples of prayer. John 17 also shows Jesus Himself at prayer, displaying intimacy with God. Prayer is ultimately what humans were made for: conversing and communicating with God. This dynamic relationship enables the Christian Disciple to engage in prayer that is both personal and relational. An action which deepens our intimacy with the God we love and follow.

However, prayer is only the penultimate stage in the relationship with God. Prayer is the forerunner of the day when the Christian Disciple will know fully, even as they are fully known (1 Corinthians 13:12). All prayer consists of a desire or longing to know God better, and that is to be our prime motivation: to know God better. That is why it is a spiritual weapon, and it is also the reason satan tries to stop Christian Disciples from praying.

Function of Prayer

The function of prayer, the act of communicating and conversing with God, reveals a constant hunger for God's help and consolidating our desire towards the ultimate goal - eternal happiness and worship and knowledge of God. It is through the Bible that desire to know God and be known by God evolves and develops. That is why prayer and Bible reading go hand in hand. Prayer emits our words from ourselves to the God we seek to know, as a response to His reaching out to us.

A popular method of prayer is the ACTS acronym. This is where prayer is described as:

- Adoration
- Confession
- Thanksgiving
- Supplication (asking – for self and others).

Through prayer, God is able to comprehend the Christian Disciple regardless of language, grammar or oratory skill, as long as the Christian Disciple approaches with a correct attitude. Words, however, are not just to be a mental action but also an emotive act, conveying emotions and feeling. Prayer is to convey deep emotions, feelings and expressions to God, regardless of our language skills. The words spoken in prayer portray our innermost feelings and desires to Him.

Because God is personal, He values language and expects His people to talk to Him. If for some reason, the Christian is unable to convey their words in prayer, then

Romans 8:26, intimates that the Holy Spirit intercedes. Prayer epitomises the Father-child relationship, which is symbolized in the Christian Disciple's relationship with God. It further symbolizes the freedom and peace in prayer, to communicate our deepest desires and yearnings.

Does God answer all prayers?

A question everybody has asked at one time or another, is "Does God answer all prayers?" First of all, the answer we expect, may not be the answer we get! So often we pray, expecting one result and getting another and then think that God hasn't answered our prayer!

Sometimes the answer He gives is 'yes'. At other times it may be 'no' or 'not yet'. When we realise that God works outside of our restrictions of time and space, we learn to trust His judgement and wisdom.

We acknowledge that He is the Master and we His servants. Alas, sometimes when we pray, we like to think we are the Master and He is our servant!

One final question: why are some prayers unanswered? There are various reasons. It could be that the prayers that aren't answered may be due to disobedience (Proverbs 28:9), doubt (James 1:5-7), pride (Luke 18:11-14), selfishness (James 4:3) or unconfessed sin (Psalm 66:18). It could just be for no reason that we can possibly see or understand at the time.

Suggested Internet Community Guidelines

Any community, regardless of size, needs guidelines. I am sure your Church community has them. Every community down through the ages has had them in one form or another. The same thing applies for those communities operating within the Internet or Digital Space, particularly those covering a global geographical base.

For any community located within Digital Space, there needs to be guidelines for both administrators and users. Without any guidelines, there would be anarchy in some form, even within communities' setup by Christians. Here is a sample of what a set of guidelines could look like for use by a Christian community on the Internet.

Guidelines for this community

a. It is our hope that this forum/community will be a place where we can serve, worship and discuss the Almighty God we love and serve, who is revealed in the Bible. As part of that, we are here to mutually encourage and enjoy the company of others on this site. This community hopefully will also act as both a hub and a haven.

b. Whilst being human, we acknowledge that over certain issues, there will be disagreements. We also acknowledge, that occasionally, different people's personalities will clash. So, bearing this in mind, we ask that in all things you would remember that Jesus is to have the supremacy over all things. This is worked out in practice by loving God and loving each other. The moderators and administrators of this site will only intervene if necessary. If you need advice about how to handle a particular event on this forum, then please do send one of them a Private Message. It will be treated confidentially.

c. Do try to be the same person in here as you would be with those offline. To do otherwise would be hypocrisy. You are also only allowed to have one identity, so please do not sign up pretending to be somebody else. That is deceitful and abusive. The only people allowed two identities are those who are administrators and they are clearly defined.

d. Respect the privacy of other people. What is said on this site, by any person, must remain on this site. Please do not copy or divulge information about another person anywhere else, without the express permission of that person. To do so, would be tantamount to gossiping.

e. People's opinions are just that: theirs! We come from different Church traditions and denominations, or none, and this is a great place to show that whilst we may differ in some areas, we are also united in acknowledging Jesus Christ who was fully God and fully human, and that He died, rose again and ascended to the right hand of the Father, so that all people everywhere may gain salvation.

Finally, this is not a conclusive list of guidelines for all scenarios of all time but rather a means of starting out as community. Additionally, if you have questions - ask! We are all here to mutually encourage and help each other, as we await that glorious day when our Saviour returns.

Index of Bible Verses

Old Testament

New Testament

About the Author

I was born in a small country town in Australia. I was raised to be a sceptical agnostic/atheist with the words "Churches are dangerous places" ringing in my ears. Coming into my teenage years, I decided if Churches are so dangerous, let's rebel and go for a bit of danger! Therefore, I rebelled, became a Christian, started attending a local Christian youth group and was baptized…

In 1990, I came to the UK for 6 months' travel around Europe! Or so I thought! I have stayed ever since. I view it as God having a sense of humour. He knows I don't like rain, cold and in particular - together! He has even given me the most beautiful of women as a wife, but she doesn't like hot weather! God sure has a sense of humour!

In 2003, I had a stroke and I took redundancy from my job. I went off to Moorlands College where I graduated in 2007. Later that year, I set up Partakers. At the end of 2019, we have had over 8 million unique visitors to the website, and had over 2 million resources downloaded. At the end of 2018, we have at a minimum of 3,500 unique visitors per day for the Podcast site.

We also now engage with others on Facebook and have an active WOWChurch engaging with people there. We also take WOWChurch into the homes of the housebound and have a number of students studying with us online at WOWBible School.

I currently reside with my wife in Bournemouth in the UK. I travel often to speak in places including the USA and Australia and would love to come and see you. I hope you have enjoyed this book and perhaps learnt something afresh or as a reminder.

Peace and blessings!

Dave.

Other Books by this Author

More titles added regularly, and all books are available in Paperback and Kindle at Amazon.

AGOG: A Glimpse Of God
An Ambassador In God's Orchestra Of Joy
Dear Christian - Get A Good Grip
Dear Church: Wake Up! Issues Facing The Church Today
Developing Intimacy With God: A Little Book Of 95 Prayers
Exploring The Bible
God Gets his Hands Dirty
God, Internet Church & You
God's WOW Words For You
Helping The Forgotten Church
Heroes And Heretics Abound
Jesus Who?
Living Life Right: Studies In Romans 12
Scriptural Delights: Exploring Psalm 119
What's It All About Alphy? The Lord's Prayer:
WOW Words Of The Bible

Glimpses Into Series:

- Leviticus: A Book Of Joy
- 1 & 2 Chronicles: Books Of Heritage And History
- Psalms: A Book Of Life
- Song Of Songs: A Book Of Relationship
- Ezekiel: A Book Of Symbols And Visions.
- The Gospels: Books Of Good News
- Acts: A Book Of Action
- Romans: A Book Of Freedom

Read This Book Series:

- Volume 1: God Of The Bible
- Volume 2: Jesus Christ
- Volume 3: Being A Christian
- Volume 4: The Church
- Volume 5: Evangelism

More titles added regularly, and all books are available in Paperback and Kindle at Amazon.
.

Helping the Forgotten Church

Who are the forgotten Church? In every community, there are people who want to attend Church, be involved in a Church, and yet for whatever reason, they are unable to. The reasons may include the demands of work. debilitating illness having to care for others or geographical isolation. This little book explores with illustrations how the Church can help these people to enjoy and participate in an interactive Church worship service. All at a time and place which is convenient for them. After all, you may one day be in need of such help, if indeed you are not already.

Available in Kindle and Paperback
ISBN: 978-1986570466
http://www.amazon.com/dp/1986570460

About Partakers

Vision Statement: Partakers exists to communicate and disseminate resources for the purposes of Christian Discipleship, Evangelism and Worship by employing radical and relevant methods, including virtual reality and online distribution.

Mission Statement: To help the world, one person at a time, to engage in whole life discipleship, as Partakers of Jesus Christ.

Contact us to see how we can help you! Seminars, coaching, preaching, teaching, discipleship or evangelism – offline or online!

> **Email:** dave@partakers.co.uk
> **Mobile:** 0794 794 5511
> **Website:** http://www.partakers.co.uk

Printed in Great Britain
by Amazon